Gloria Steinem:
90 Remarkable Tales From
90 Extraordinary Years

A Lifetime of Lessons and Stories

Anthony Dobbs

Table of Contents

For my girls, Charlie and Lola. Your voices are powerful and your dreams are limitless. Continue to speak your truth and envision a world where equality knows no bounds. May you always find the courage to challenge injustice, the compassion to lift others, and the resilience to pursue your dreams fearlessly.

Trigger warning: This book contains mention of abortion, rape, and similar topics that might be triggering to certain readers.

Introduction

We are linked, not ranked. –Gloria Steinem

This short and extremely powerful quote perfectly encapsulates everything that Gloria Steinem has been fighting for her entire life. The story behind it is as inspiring as the quote itself. Gloria is an advisory board member of the trailblazing magazine *Feminist.com*, and in 2013, was asked to create a bracelet as part of Maiden Nation's campaign with Yoko Ono. When asked to come up with a phrase that could fit on the bracelet, she chose the one above. The bracelet carried this quote on one side, and the word "Imagine" on the other. It became extremely popular, especially in Steinem's interactions with icons like Ruth Bader Ginsburg. In 2015, when her memoir *Life on the Road* was published, it comprised a slightly different version of this quote, "When humans are ranked instead of linked, everyone loses."

At 90, Steinem is just as vocal and enthusiastic a supporter of women's and human rights as she was when she started out. In fact, she acknowledges that this is a time of both "danger and promise at the same time." As both the feminist and human rights movements face fresh and complex challenges, Steinem is still very much on the scene—encouraging young activists and thinkers and urging them to show up every day for the causes they believe in.

The world we live in today has changed a lot from the world in which Steinem first started her journalism and activism career—in both good and bad ways. We're now at a tipping point in history, where our actions and beliefs will shape the future of this world in various ways. As adults, we need to fight our fatigue and jaded attitude to see the world for the beautiful and chaotic place it is. At the same time, we want our tweens and teens to grow up in a world where their existence is celebrated instead of tolerated. Lucky for us, Steinem's voice still acts as a powerful and compassionate guide to all of us. This book is both an ode to Steinem's tireless activism over the years and a message of hope to anyone who wants to embark on their own journey of creating meaningful change in their lives.

Steinem's journey is noteworthy because even though her origins lie in second-wave feminism—and she has done a lot to contribute to its success—she has also participated in conversations around intersectional feminism throughout the world. As someone who has traveled extensively throughout her life, Steinem has used those experiences to become aware of the challenges that women face in different cultural contexts and use it to expand the scope of "traditional" feminism in the Western world.

As someone with such a storied career and life, it's impossible that Steinem hasn't faced her fair share of controversies and challenges. Through this book, we'll get to know more about the challenges she faced in her life and how she's used them to evolve over the years. Not only that, but we'll also get to know the many friends and allies who have stood by her and helped her overcome these obstacles.

This is a great book for anyone interested in history or biographies of influential personalities. It's also an interesting way to understand one of the most popular, complex, and interesting figures of second-wave feminism in the US and the world. Last but not least, these short but remarkable tales will help anyone who is either starting a career in activism or who wants a fresh boost of energy to keep going on this journey.

Gloria Steinem: 90 Remarkable Tales From 90 Extraordinary Years hopes to retell the remarkable story of Gloria Steinem as a young girl, woman, daughter, friend, feminist, storyteller, and organizer. Each of these 90 stories will help us become intimate with the details of her childhood, her early foray into journalism, and the challenges she faced while trying to find her voice as a feminist, activist, and writer. We'll rejoice in her triumphs, commiserate over her setbacks, and witness her growth as a beacon for lasting change. In the end, we'll also learn about the legacy she leaves behind and the advice she has for those of us who are still figuring out our path in life.

Chapter 1:

Early Life—Lessons at Home and

Beyond

Gloria Steinem—born on March 25, 1934—was the second and youngest daughter of her parents Leo and Ruth Steinem. Her older sister, Susanne, was nine years older than her. Gloria was born in Toledo, Ohio, in the United States—which was where both her parents had been born and also where they had both studied (at the University of Toledo). She had a rather unconventional, sometimes challenging, but often enlightening childhood. As someone who has traveled extensively, she experienced both the joys and challenges of living an itinerant life.

1. Lessons on the Road as a Child

Gloria grew up for the most part in Michigan, where her father, Leo, ran a "summer resort" that was more like a dance pavilion known as the "Ocean Beach Pier." During these months, her mother, Ruth, supported her husband in various ways. For the rest of the year, Gloria spent most of her time on the road with her parents.

Life on the road was full of uncertainty and challenges, especially for a young girl. While her teenage sister was able to enroll in high schools that were close to where they stayed for the time being, Gloria did not go to school until she started living with her mother after her parents' divorce. However, this period in her life taught her many things. For one, she discovered her love for books and reading. In fact, she first learned to read through the various road signs she encountered on her journeys.

It was during these travels that Gloria learned to work with her father—looking for antiques in country auctions and selling them to roadside dealers for a profit. Every member of the family contributed to the family's finances, and Gloria learned from a very young age to play her part in this system. While her mother was responsible for determining the price at which they should sell the antiques, Susanne sold popcorn in the summer from a stand given to her by her father and Gloria learned to wrap and unwrap the items that her father bought at the auctions.

She also witnessed two things during this time that would shape her understanding of travel as well as her father. She realized that her father was so drawn to the road that he would often ask them to leave the house and get into the car with little to no preparation. This meant that they barely got to stay home but also that her father resisted giving in to the "allure" of home. This created a lot of strain on her mother and became one of the reasons for both the divorce and her mother's mental health struggles.

What she also realized was that these travels were the first time she found a place in a world where there was no certainty and no real concept of home. She learned to appreciate the kindness and guidance of strangers along the way—the people who made life easier for those on the road. One of her strongest and fondest memories of these childhood travels was of the times when they traveled along the sea. She began to see these moments as moments of deep connection with the world around her—something that encouraged her to travel more as a young adult.

2. Challenges Faced in Her Childhood

While Gloria had many fond memories of her childhood, she also experienced something that she would not admit to herself until much later. During this period, Gloria longed for a place she could call home.

She was inspired by movies that depicted a conventional family living peacefully in a well-maintained house. This was, of course, very different from her reality, and she did not think of her life as something to aspire to.

Her challenges increased considerably when her parents divorced. While she understood that her parents were better off separately, it also meant that she had to become her mother's primary caretaker. She was 10 at this time, and her sister was already off to college. When their summer resort closed down permanently, her father had to spend almost all his time on the road and he was unable to take care of Ruth anymore. This meant that, from the time she was 10 to when she left for college at 17, Gloria lived alone with her mother—first in a small town close to where her sister studied, and then in Toledo, in her mother's ancestral home.

This period could be excruciating at times, especially because the house they lived in was in disrepair, and it was also a place where Ruth—reminded of her own difficult childhood—experienced severe mental health issues. During this period, Gloria had to deal with instances where her mother didn't remember things and even sent the police to look for Gloria when she was at her after-school job. On one hand, she constantly worried for her mother, especially as she needed to hold down part-time jobs to support them both. On the other hand, she had trouble having empathy for her mother because she pitied her and she was sometimes ashamed of her mother's condition.

At the same time, it would be unfair to think of this period as a solely dark one. On the contrary, this period gave Gloria a chance to bond with her mother and to start seeing her as an individual, instead of as only a loving and kind mother who kept their household going despite her husband's eccentricities. This was where, for Gloria, a different portrait of her mother emerged—one that would help her appreciate the struggles that women faced even after the relative success of first-wave feminism.

3. Her Father's Influence on Her Life

Gloria was able to see her father as a complex person. This complexity didn't particularly arise from what he said or did because he had always been a traveler at heart. He had never wanted or understood a conventional life and everything he did was in sync with those beliefs. Gloria also understood, perhaps when she grew a bit older, how her father's lifestyle had created immense challenges for her mother. While she didn't resent her father, she initially tried to live a life that was entirely opposite to his. She craved stability and security, which meant that she almost gave in to the allure of a conventional life.

Still, the things she realized as she grew up was that she shared her father's love for travel and autonomy. As a child, Gloria sometimes hoped that she was actually adopted and that her real family would come and take her away from the life her father had created for them. As she grew up, however, she began to understand the allure of traveling, meeting new people, and expanding her definition of what life could be like. She remembered that her father took pride in never having a job where he had to be accountable to anyone else. As an adult, she found herself repeating similar patterns when she resigned from a remote job that later became a hybrid one.

One of her greatest regrets as a young adult was not being there for her father in his last moments. Since she was traveling when her father got into an accident and was hospitalized, she was only able to reach the hospital after he had passed away. Later, she took solace in the fact that two of his closest friends had been there for him during this time, but she still regretted the many things she could not explicitly thank him for—things she would always be grateful to him for.

She loved her father for not caring so much about rules as much as about her happiness in the moment. While her father's unconventional parenting methods didn't always inspire confidence, they did help her become far more independent than most children her age. She also loved that her father was a kind and loving man. As a young adult, she saw how other women were attracted to men who didn't treat them well, simply because they had never seen what a kind man looked like.

For Gloria, kindness and gentleness became almost prerequisites in the men she was attracted to or even those she considered her friends. Her father, thus, gave her a wonderful example of what a good man could be.

One of the most significant examples of how her father's kindness impacted those around him came from a letter she received from retired obstetrician, John Grover, who used to be a part of a band that performed at their summer resort. In his letter, he told Gloria how her father's kindness had saved him and his bandmate from homelessness during one summer and how he would always be grateful to her father for that. Interestingly, Grover found it serendipitous that he had also been involved in fighting for the reproductive rights of women in Massachusetts—a fight that Gloria herself was deeply involved in.

Gloria believes that she received her optimism for a better world from her father, whose boundless enthusiasm and belief in the inherent goodness of the world helped combat some of the fears and insecurities she had inherited when taking care of her mother and facing uncertainty as a child.

4. The Portrait of a Mother and the Makings of a Young Feminist

Gloria's relationship with her mother was complicated, not least because she didn't really meet the woman her mother was before she gave birth to her, until much later in her life. Her mother had suffered her first "nervous breakdown" before Gloria was born and when her sister was 5 years old. When she returned from the sanatorium where she stayed after this breakdown, she was almost always under the shadow of anxiety and depression. She was usually scared of being alone, unable to travel on her own, and needing sedatives to sleep. However, this doesn't mean that she didn't care for her two children as best she could.

In fact, she was determined to not repeat the pain that her own mother had inflicted on her when she was growing up. She was able to make her daughters feel loved and protected to the best of her abilities. After Ruth's childhood home was finally demolished, Susanne asked their father to stay and take care of her mother for a year so that Gloria could go to school in Washington, D.C., with her and have a chance at a normal school year for once. After that, however, Ruth's condition deteriorated to a point where she needed full-time care. Susanne could not manage both work and full-time caregiving responsibilities, so she found a good hospital in Baltimore—where their mother was able to get good care and where her condition improved enough for Gloria to be able to see who her mother really was.

During her visits to Baltimore—and even in Toledo—she heard many stories from her mother that helped her understand her mother's pain, disappointment, and various qualities. Her mother had been a trailblazer in her own right, despite the fact that she didn't get a lot of support from her own mother. She loved reading and basketball, drove her uncle's Stanley Steamer when no other woman in her neighborhood did, and even defied her mother and went to dances that the church did not support. She got into Oberlin College but had to return home when her mother didn't have enough money to send her there. When she joined the University of Toledo, she met Leo and decided to marry him. He was a kind man and was very different from her mother and the life she was trying to leave behind.

Gloria also came to know that her mother had worked as a journalist even after giving birth to Susanne, and she became the Sunday editor in a reputed Toledo daily. This was extremely unusual for her time, especially as a married woman with a young kid. During this time, she also realized that her husband, though kind, wasn't able to provide her the support she needed as a young mother. Since her husband was almost always traveling, she was left to worry about the practical aspects of their life. She also came to terms with the fact that she loved journalism a lot and considered leaving her husband to pursue a career and life of her own. Ultimately, she didn't because she was conscious of how society viewed her and because she felt guilty at the thought of putting her husband and daughters through something like that.

Nevertheless, the pressures of balancing her career and family without any real help—and the consequent pain of having to sacrifice herself for the sake of her husband's dreams—finally got to her and probably stayed with her throughout most of her life. Her time in Baltimore, however, brought hope into all their lives and helped Gloria see her mother in a new light. It also helped her appreciate the challenges her mother had faced and the ways in which she had tried to shelter her daughters from her pain. After this period, Ruth began to live more independently—though almost never alone—and discovered and rediscovered many of the things that made her who she was. Her relationship with Gloria and Susanne was not without its ups and downs but she proved herself to be a dedicated and loving mother at various points, like when she sold her Toledo house in order to ensure Gloria's college education.

Perhaps, the most enlightening and heartbreaking interaction she had with her mother was when they were talking about the choices Ruth had to make for the rest of her life. This was when she was contemplating leaving for New York to try and have a solid journalism career. When Gloria urged her mother to say why she didn't make that choice and why she didn't choose the life she was meant to live—her mother told her that if she had, Gloria would never have been born. At that moment, and for a long time after that, Gloria believed that this choice might have ensured that *Ruth* was born—in other words, it could have been a chance for her to be who she truly was. It was also one of the first times that Gloria understood what a woman could stand to lose if she had to put her role as a mother (or would-be mother) over her aspirations as an individual.

5. The Path Not Taken and the Life Not Lived

In another life, Gloria could have been an extremely well-known dancer—enthralling audiences worldwide with her performances. Even though we know Gloria as an amazing writer, feminist, and organizer today, she did indulge in her passion for dance as a child and even as a college student. She first learned to tap dance at her father's resort in Michigan. When she lived with her mother in Toledo, Gloria had to single-handedly take care of her—which took its toll on her. Not only that, but she also had to handle comments made by the people around her about her mother. At this time, her father used to write to her every now and then but they only made his absence that much more obvious.

To keep herself busy and distract herself from the harsh realities of life, Gloria joined an after-school tap dancing class. At the time, she thought that only women in show business were doing something different, and dance seemed like a way out. Not only did she enjoy it but she became so good at it that she started dancing at operettas and earning up to ten dollars per night. Of course, tap dancing could not provide permanent relief from her struggles, but it helped her develop a lifelong passion for dance. Even today, Gloria loves to dance whenever she can.

6. Learning About Women's Health Through Her Mother's Challenges

Before Ruth received the care in Baltimore that she should have gotten much earlier, her extended family tried to help her in whatever way they could. Most of the doctors they went to recommended admitting her to mental hospitals, but those weren't always the best places for women to improve their mental health. Other times, Ruth's own family would dismiss and diminish her mother's concerns.

What Gloria realized over time was that her mother wasn't considered "an important worker" by society, which was a fate that most women shared at the time. She realized that her mother's case was not unique; in fact, it was all too common. Women like her mother had to handle a lot of challenges in a society that was still patriarchal in many ways. Not only that, but they were not given the help they needed and deserved because the heartbreaking truth was that they didn't matter as much as men. This realization also laid the foundation for Gloria's later work as a journalist and activist.

7. Pauline Perlmutter Steinem and Gloria's Link to Feminism

Gloria was certainly not the first feminist in her family. Her paternal grandmother—Pauline Perlmutter Steinem—was an influential figure during the era of first-wave feminism. She was the first ever woman board member of a school in Ohio, she had supported suffragist movements, and had even addressed Congress. She had also helped her family members escape Nazi Germany when the war started. Gloria was only 5 when she passed away, so she did not get to know her too well, but she did get to know her through her mother's stories. In fact, she also understood that her mother idolized Pauline and was closer to her than her own mother.

Despite much evidence as to her courage, Gloria felt perplexed by one thing: She was unable to understand why Pauline had not helped Ruth overcome her challenges and helped her carve a life for herself. If anyone could have encouraged her mother to become her own person, it was Pauline, and yet this didn't seem to be the case. Gloria later realized that while Pauline had been a staunch feminist when it came to securing the vote and the right to work for women, her brand of feminism ended outside her own home. In fact, she was more often than not sacrificing her own needs and principles in order to appease her husband and maybe even her sons. Her father too, Gloria realized, though extremely kind and generous in many ways, was not a feminist in the absolute sense. He didn't make it easier for his wife to pursue her passions and dreams, didn't let her drive, and wanted her to give up her job in order to support his dreams and take care of the household.

Gloria believed that her grandmother could have contributed to Ruth's guilt by taking care of the household and always being able to fulfill everyone else's demands. The realization that first-wave feminism, though extremely important, had its limitations helped Gloria become one of the leading voices of second-wave feminism.

Chapter 2:

Early Career as a Journalist—

Finding and Fighting for Her Voice

Gloria had always envisioned a life in writing—right from the days when she devoured Louisa May Alcott's books as a young girl on the road with her family—but she had no idea how she would accomplish that. After graduating magna cum laude from Smith College in 1956, she left for India on the Chester Bowles Asian Fellowship for two years. This experience laid the foundation for her career as a journalist and an organizer and also helped Gloria understand the importance of intersectionality and communal spaces when organizing movements.

8. Lessons in India—Beginnings in Journalism and Organizing

Traveling through India right after college was both a culture shock and an awakening for Gloria. It took her a while to adjust to the chaotic way of life there, but she came away with not only stories and friends but also a very different view of how movements could be realized throughout the world. As someone who took a keen interest in investigative journalism when she officially started her career in New York, Gloria benefited immensely from traveling through India the way most locals did. She learned a lot about the remarkable lives of ordinary Indians—especially Indian women—when traveling with them on buses and on the life-changing train journey she took from Kolkata to Kerala. During this trip, she began to shed many of the preconceived notions about Indian women—especially those who were uneducated and primarily living in villages—that were common not only in Western media but also among the well-educated, elite Indians.

One of the most intriguing things she learned was that these women understood how too many pregnancies were adversely affecting their bodies. When Indira Gandhi, the country's first female Prime Minister, eventually introduced family planning programs, many of the urban elite thought it would not be easy to convince them, but the women proved them wrong.

Another lesson she learned during this period was related to the power of community when organizing movements at one of the *ashrams* of Vinoba Bhave—who is considered by many as Mahatma Gandhi's spiritual successor. Here, she learned about the value of nonviolence as well as the power of listening to the people. She understood the importance of meeting people in their spaces and forming connections with them before trying to effect change in their lives. Most importantly, she experienced the magic of "talking circles"—where everyone was invited to talk about their experiences and there was no real hierarchy among the people—a concept that became a part of her life when she became a traveling feminist organizer in the future.

She also launched her journalism career in India by writing for Indian newspapers and providing a foreigner's view on Indian culture. She wrote to *The Saturday Evening Post* in hopes of being able to write more articles about Indian culture, but ultimately, she wasn't commissioned by them. However, she did publish a series of articles in *The Sophian*, which was Smith's independent, student-run newspaper. In these articles, she wrote about the politics of the region—like the Kashmir issue—from an Indian perspective and also focused on the various social customs of India. She focused on the traditional system of arranged marriages in India and on the vibrant wedding customs she witnessed firsthand as a student at Miranda House at Delhi University. When she came back from India, she had a wealth of experiences and a strong understanding of the kind of stories she wanted to tell.

9. Challenges Faced as a Woman in Journalism

Upon her return from India, Gloria went to New York, aspiring to be a journalist. She wanted to report on human-interest and political stories—something that she had already gotten a taste of back in India. However, in the 1960s, it was extremely difficult for women to be assigned to pieces that were not focused on food, fashion, dating, or general lifestyle. This was a tricky period for Gloria because, on the one hand, she was living her (and her mother's) dream of becoming a journalist in New York and making a living as a freelance writer but on the other hand, she had to write pieces that she didn't believe in.

Some of the pieces she wrote during that time included "Crazy Legs Or, The Biography of a Fashion," based on the popularity of textured stockings among women at the time, and "How to Find Your Type," a piece on helping women decode their personal style and living according to it. Another notable piece she wrote at the time was called "Funny Ways to Find a Man on the Beach," which dispensed advice such as "look different," "look the same only better," and "make him think he did it."

She considers the piece on textured stockings as one of the low points of her career and also rues her "lack of spine" (Leland, 2016) but also acknowledges that she had to write these pieces to ensure she could pay her rent. Decades after doing these pieces, however, Gloria felt that some of these topics were actually interesting and should be taken up by male editors as well—not least because women aren't always the sole authority on fashion and lifestyle and because women have been challenging their identities and roles for a long time.

An interesting thing to note about her time as a fledgling journalist is that Gloria doesn't put the blame entirely on her editors for her failure to write pieces that she was passionate about. In fact, she has talked about how it took her many years to become the writer and journalist she wanted to be, and one of the reasons for that was that she felt she needed to assist men or stay in their shadows rather than assert herself in meetings. She spent a long time doing research for the men in her team or willingly passing on her ideas to them because she believed that they would be taken more seriously if they came from a man rather than a woman. Even if some of the men she encountered wouldn't be intimidated by the presence of a strong and intelligent woman, it was difficult for her to overcome her own conditioning.

10. *Esquire*—and Her First Serious Assignment as a Journalist

Gloria's grit paid off when, in 1962, she was commissioned by Clay Felker—features editor for *Esquire Magazine*—for a piece on contraception. This was her first serious assignment and it took a while for her to get it right. The piece—titled "The Moral Disarmament of Betty Coed" (Steinem, 1962)—tackled issues related to the sexual revolution and liberation of women in the aftermath of the usage of the contraceptive pill becoming more widespread in the United States. This piece highlighted how the meaning and implications of sex were changing for both men and women, the challenges that women still dealt with, and the effect that contraception had on women's careers and lives.

Based on her research, Gloria wrote about some interesting shifts in perception at the time. The most important one was that the young women of that time didn't define themselves by who they had sex with and why. In fact, they had begun to see sex as a neutral thing, and they had become more individual about their choices—not deferring to popular opinions around sex and marriage. To not have themselves defined solely by their sexual activities was liberating for these women, and they began to see it as a part of their own growth and development process.

Gloria also talked about how an increase in education and income made women more prone to using contraception and even assuming responsibility for their own protection. Gloria also talked about how the introduction of the pill helped women own their sexual desires because they were no longer burdened by the thought of unintended consequences. In this piece, psychologists also talked about how contraception had made it so that women didn't have to choose between marriage and a career and had given rise to the "self-motivated and autonomous" girl.

This piece also examined certain hypocrisies that might have arisen due to the changed attitudes of society after contraception became popular. For instance, she talked about how some women might be encouraged to pretend to want sex before marriage or to become career women rather than housewives—even if that's what they truly wanted. At the same time, it was becoming clear that women didn't really have an "anatomy of destiny"—a phrase coined by Sigmund Freud to talk about how women were tied to certain characteristics and behaviors simply because they were built that way. In fact, women could be who they chose to be, and it was actually society that might have been conditioning women to fulfill certain roles over others.

The last part of this article shone a light on what could have been the *real* obstacle to women's true liberation—the fact that men might not be able to keep pace with women's liberation and might have difficulty changing their own perspectives of how women should work, marry, love, and live.

11. *Show* Magazine—and an Exceptional Undercover Assignment

Gloria always wanted to do work that was true to her vision of being a journalist, and she got that opportunity when she was assigned, in 1963, by *Show* magazine to carry out an undercover assignment as a Playboy Bunny. She assumed the pen name Marie Ochs and responded to an ad by the New York Playboy Club for Playboy Bunnies. At the time, the club advertised that attractive girls between the ages of 18 and 24 could become Bunnies and enjoy a life of glamor and excitement. Not only that, but they were promised a weekly salary of $200–$300— something they claimed was difficult even for secretaries at prestigious organizations to earn. Gloria decided to become a Playboy Bunny in order to understand how these clubs operated and whether their claims were, in fact, true.

Published in two parts, the article—titled "A Bunny's Tale" (Steinem, 1963)—highlighted Gloria's experiences as a Bunny, and also exposed the working conditions prevalent in these clubs. She wrote about the "Bunny Bible," which listed all the rules that Bunnies needed to follow, as well as the actions that would lead to various "demerits." She also found out that the Bunnies were made to wear high heels at all times (wearing medium heels would lead to a demerit), stuff their bosoms in order to look a certain way, and even undergo examinations to check for venereal diseases. While, on the surface, all measures were taken to ensure that the customers at the club did not get into any sort of relationships with the Bunnies, exceptions were made for the "Number One Keyholders"—which not only included Playboy executives but even certain members of the press.

During the three weeks that Gloria was employed as a Bunny, she gleaned lots of insights about the miserable working conditions at the club as well as the false promises made by the club regarding the amount that a Bunny could earn per week. In fact, she realized that between the amount that the club took from the tips she made and the amount she needed to spend on maintaining her appearance—she was severely underpaid. She battled fatigue, extreme weight loss (due to a costume so tight that it would "give a man a cleavage"), and borderline harassment by the predominantly male clientele at the club to help uncover the truth of how the Bunnies were really treated at these clubs.

12. The Impact of and Fallout From *A Bunny's Tale*

This article was an amazing achievement for Gloria, both as a journalist and a feminist in the making. It revealed the lies that Hugh Hefner's Playboy empire and brand had peddled, so much so that Gloria was sued by them for defamation. More importantly, though, it helped readers come to terms with how the "sexually liberated" lifestyle that

Hefner promoted at the time had nothing to do with empowering women and everything to do with appealing to the male gaze.

However, the article also created problems for Gloria, whose journalism career had only just begun picking up speed. She talked about how she was seen as a lesser and unserious reporter because she was a "Bunny," no matter the reasons behind it. Also, the photos that were taken during her time as a Bunny haunted her for a long time. It became difficult for Gloria to get new work, especially of a more serious nature. In fact, as Gloria's stature as a journalist, feminist, and activist grew over the years, her detractors used this article—and her stint as a Bunny—to question her credibility.

Over the years, however, Gloria understood why this article was important. She is now proud of having done this assignment and of exposing the practices of a place that essentially thrived on the objectification and labor of young women.

13. The Abortion Speak-Out of 1969 and Coming Into Her Own as a Feminist

Gloria believes that she did not begin her "life as an active feminist" until the day she covered an abortion speak-out held in the basement of the Washington Square Methodist Church in Greenwich Village in New York. This was a time when abortion was still illegal and *Roe v. Wade* was years from being established. There were very few cases in which women were allowed to get an abortion and the decisions—both at the government as well as the medical levels—almost exclusively belonged to men. In fact, a hearing held to debate the legalization of abortion consisted of fourteen men and one nun. Not only were women not being given a chance to speak, but those who did get to speak often rallied against abortion rights.

Women had become tired and angry at not having a say in matters related to their own reproductive health and decided to talk openly about their experiences with abortion as part of a women-only gathering. Gloria had, by then, started a job with *New York* magazine—which was started by Clay Felker, her editor at *Esquire*. In 1969, she was present at the speak-out as a reporter, and she couldn't help but be inspired by the women taking control of their narratives around abortion.

Gloria, who was at the time in her mid-30s, had undergone an abortion herself when she was 22. She had just graduated from college and was engaged to a man she respected but didn't want to marry. Since she was pregnant, her future looked bleak. Gloria broke off her engagement when she left for India, but on the way, she decided to seek the help of a doctor who would perform an abortion on her. This man—whose name was Dr. John Sharpe—was a British physician. At the time, the only reason that physicians in England could perform an abortion was if the woman's health was in danger. However, Sharpe decided to perform an abortion on a woman he didn't know and who wasn't in any health-related danger. In return for this, he asked her to promise him two things: one, that she would not mention his name to anyone, and two, that she would live her life on her own terms. Years after his death, Gloria broke the first promise by dedicating her 2015 memoir *My Life on the Road* to him.

Reflecting on the emotions surrounding her decision to abort as a 22-year-old woman, Gloria felt that though she was conditioned to feel guilt over her decision, she never felt that way. In fact, she realized that her life was her own and that she couldn't afford to not do it. While she felt positive about her abortion decision, she wasn't able to own it and talk about it openly with others—until she witnessed these women at the speak-out. She felt a "big click" (*Gloria Steinem*, n.d.) when she saw women take themselves and their issues seriously and it gave her the courage to own her own past experiences as well.

This was also where she realized that men's problems were taken more seriously than women's issues. She quotes a person who had said this to her, "Honey, if men could get pregnant, abortion would be a sacrament" (Brockes, 2015)—and even today asserts how chillingly true this statement is.

14. The Article That Solidified Gloria's Position as the Leader of Second-Wave Feminism

On April 7, 1969, Gloria Steinem wrote and published an article in the "City Politic" column of the *New York Times* (Steinem, 1969). This was a groundbreaking article in which Gloria talked about the Women's Liberation Movement and its evolution over the ages. She discussed how women were finally taking charge of their lives and even challenging the basic idea of liberation in people's minds.

This article was revolutionary in many ways. For one, it talked about how first-wave feminism had allowed women the right to vote and to work, but it had not accounted for the various challenges that women still faced in the outside world. She discussed issues such as the wage gap, the discrimination against women at every level, and the different kinds of legislation that were only meant to "protect men" from the consequences of having women in the workplace.

This piece also highlighted the invisible forces that kept women either confined to their homes or disillusioned them at their workplaces. She talked about the effects of women not receiving adequate help and support after childbirth and the blame and criticism they had to endure when they ventured out on their own. At the same time, this article was not morose in any way. If anything, it showed the readers how women all across the country were organizing and taking matters into their own hands.

The most striking aspect of this article, however, was its attempt at intersectional feminism. This article discussed certain similarities between the ways in which Black men were treated by White men and the ways in which women, in general, were treated by men. She came to the radical conclusion that women of different classes might have more in common with each other than men and women of the same class or race. She also talked about how the women's movement could become more empathetic and inclusive by understanding the struggles of women who belong to the lower socioeconomic classes.

In this article, Gloria referenced *The Feminine Mystique*—a groundbreaking book written by Betty Friedan and published in 1963—which is considered one of the foundational texts of second-wave feminism. Interestingly, Gloria's article has since become a part of the second-wave feminist canon as well.

Chapter 3:

Second-Wave Feminism, Ms. Magazine, and Gloria's Journey as a Feminist Leader

After the 1969 article was published in *New York* magazine, Gloria came into her own as a feminist leader, organizer, and writer. Up to this point, she had largely been an observer rather than an active participant in many aspects of her career and life. This was due, in part, to her experiences as a child and young adult. Having been solely responsible for her mother's welfare at various points growing up, Gloria didn't want to be responsible for other people's welfare as an adult. Because of this experience, she wanted to stay as independent as possible in terms of her career and her life as a whole. Of course, life had other plans for her and she soon found herself at the center of the country's feminist movement.

15. The Founding of *Ms.* Magazine: The First National American Feminist Magazine

Ms. magazine started at a time when feminism was struggling to find a place in mainstream society. At the time, the media either ridiculed or ignored feminism as a movement and only catered to the accepted concerns of women of finding a husband, wearing the right clothes or cosmetics, and raising children. In 1970, feminist groups tried to take over the magazine *Ladies Home Journal*, complaining that it focused exclusively on housekeeping and ignored real issues that could have an impact on women's rights. This was a problem with almost all the magazines at the time.

At this time, Gloria was trying to raise funds for the Women's Action Alliance—which was a feminist educational organization she had founded the same year with Brenda Feigen-Fasteau and Dorothy Pitman Hughes.

Gloria and her fellow feminist partners realized that there was a lack of media for women *by* women, and initially, she thought that a newsletter would be a great idea in order to reach these women and raise funds for their case. However, Brenda—who was also the national vice-president of the National Organization of Women at the time—encouraged Gloria to invest instead in a glossy magazine. While Gloria was a bit unsure about the demand for such a magazine, Brenda assured her that there was.

At the time, Gloria was working at *New York* magazine with Clay Felker, and this allowed her and her cofounders—Patricia Carbine and Elizabeth Forsling Harris—to launch *Ms.* magazine as a one-shot, 40-page insert in *New York* magazine's December 1971 issue.

16. Obstacles and Criticisms Faced Before, During, and After the Launch of *Ms.*

The road to publication was beset with challenges and difficulties. On one hand, the magazine had to contend with male columnists and journalists who were not only skeptical about the magazine's success but also ridiculed the feminist sentiment behind its launch. On reading through a preview issue of the magazine, columnist James J. Kilpatrick called it a "note of petulance, of bitchiness, or nervous fingernails screeching across a blackboard" (*About Ms.*, 2023).

When the one-shot became popular enough to warrant a regular issue in 1972, news anchor Henry Reasoner gave it six months before it ran out of things to say. Republicans were expectedly furious, and they responded by banning the magazine from public libraries and by condemning it on record. In fact, President Nixon also poked fun at Gloria and indicated that people hardly knew her and didn't care about what she had to say through her magazine. Its covers also drew criticism every now and then and were used as reasons to boycott particular issues. Over time, the editors decided to tone down the covers to pacify librarians and advertisers. According to Gloria, some people criticized the magazine because they didn't understand feminism, while others criticized it because they did.

Even though Clay Felker was instrumental in the launch of the magazine, he wasn't always in agreement with Gloria regarding the feminist issues that were discussed in it. Intriguingly, this magazine also faced some criticism from liberals and feminists. While some—like the radical feminist group Redstockings—didn't like that there were no "established voices" from the alternative publishing scene in the magazine, others thought it was not radical enough. Still, there were others who thought that it was too individualistic and career-focused, and many even believed it was too capitalistic in its vision and too glossy to be a serious magazine.

A pertinent point of contention regarding the magazine was that, despite the editor's attempts to cater to diverse readers, it failed to do so. While there were attempts every once in a while to include people of color in the issues, it was predominantly a magazine focused on White people.

Another major issue *Ms.* faced in its initial years was finding the right advertisers. Gloria had to deal with a lot of sexist behavior and stereotyping when she tried to talk to potential advertisers. For instance, the head of a major cosmetics company told her that the average reader of *Ms.* wasn't into makeup, while the executives of car manufacturing companies in Detroit told her that if women began to drive cars, the value of those cars would go down.

17. Important Decisions Related to *Ms.*

Gloria and her cofounders made two main decisions regarding the magazine. The first one was the name of the magazine. Before settling on the current name, the editors toyed with names like "Lilith," "Bimbo," and "Sisters." When they finally decided to choose the name *Ms.* instead of "Miss" or "Mrs.," they had to include an explanation for the readers. They decided to choose the name *Ms.* to remove any connotations regarding the marital status of women. They wanted to emphasize the autonomy of a woman and her identity outside the confines of marriage.

Another important decision made by Gloria and the editors was to keep the management of the magazine women- and feminist-focused. They did this by refusing to allow advertisements that were sexist in nature or those where the advertisers pressured the editors to include content relevant to the products being advertised. They realized that this would be contrary to the spirit of the magazine.

While the magazine had to deal with various financial and creative pressures, the editors also experimented with different organizational structures and formats. For instance, it sometimes operated as a nonprofit organization, while at other times, it was supported by different commercial owners who allowed the magazine to remain free of advertisements for a considerable duration.

18. Important Milestones Reached by *Ms.* Magazine

Ever since the inception of the magazine, Gloria—along with her entire team—made it a point to tackle issues that were largely absent from mainstream media—including thorny issues such as domestic violence, sexual harassment, and abortion. *Ms.* became the first magazine to center the voices of American women who demanded that abortion be made legal. It also featured a weekly "No Comment" section where readers of the magazine called out any misogynistic advertisements they saw around them. Interestingly, it also began the practice of rating presidential candidates based on their focus on women's issues.

The initial one-shot issue—with only 300,000 copies—sold out within eight days. Gloria was also on a radio show in California when a reader called and told her that they were unable to find the issue anywhere. That is when Clay Felker informed her that all those copies had sold out, proving to her and many others that there was a rather enthusiastic audience for a feminist magazine.

An interesting thing about the first official issue of the magazine—which was released in 1972—was that it featured Wonder Woman on the cover (its title was "Wonder Woman for President"). One of the main reasons for this decision was that DC Comics—the publisher of *Wonder Woman*—had recently decided to take away all her superpowers. This caused *Ms.* to focus on the character's history and her contributions toward the cause of feminism. What's even more amazing is that their efforts contributed, at least in part, to DC's decision to restore Wonder Woman's superpowers.

As impressive as the sales figures of the magazine were, they weren't the only measure of its success. The one-shot issue prompted readers to send in over 20,000 personal letters to the editors, most of them talking about the impact that the issue had on them. The editors have continued to receive these letters throughout the history of *Ms.*, and they have also taken into account the criticism offered by some of their readers and used them to improve their forthcoming issues.

To Gloria, *Ms.* represented a victory on the personal, professional, and political levels. An interesting thing that happened because of her involvement with *Ms.* was that she became responsible for the welfare of her colleagues and employees and did not feel burdened by it. This was a far cry from the young woman who did not want to be responsible for anyone else in her life.

19. Gloria's Reflections on the Impact of *Ms.* Over 50 Years of Publication

In the fifty years since its first publication, *Ms.* has achieved many firsts. To commemorate its fifty years in print, a book was released by Knopf Publishing, titled *50 Years of Ms.: The Best of the Pathfinding Magazine That Ignited a Revolution* (Steinem, 2023)—which contained a foreword by Gloria. In it, Gloria talked about the challenges faced by her team during the inception of the magazine, as well as about the highlights of her journey with the publication. She admitted that even she could not have predicted that it would remain relevant 50 years later.

At the same time, she admitted that a lot of work still needs to be done in order to make true equality possible. She placed her faith in future generations—calling herself a "hopeaholic" (Braver, 2023)—and urged them to imagine what they wanted to create.

20. *Women Alive!* and the Feminist Majority Foundation—Keeping the Spirit of *Ms.* Alive

In 1974, the magazine's editors decided to produce a television program to extend its reach. The program came to be known as *Women Alive!* It contained documentary pieces, interviews, comedy sketches, and even entertainment pieces that concerned themselves with issues related to women's empowerment. Most of the short documentaries and entertainment pieces were made by independent women filmmakers and women connected to the performing arts.

In the pilot episode, Gloria was interviewed at the offices of the magazine. Not only that, but she also narrated a round-table discussion with members of the National Black Feminist Organization. The pilot also included Black women and women belonging to the working class in a bid to be more diverse. Throughout its run, the show attempted to celebrate women and highlight the issues faced by them in various aspects of life.

A major challenge faced by *Ms.* over the years was in finding investors and owners who truly believed in their mission. Their search was finally over in 2001 when the magazine was sold to the Feminist Majority Foundation. The organization was founded in 1987 by Eleanor Smeal, Katherine Spillar, Peg Yorkin, Toni Carabillo, and Judith Meuli, and its aim was to raise and nurture the feminist consciousness across the nation. The founders truly believed that both men and women could be feminists and that feminists were, in fact, the majority in the United States. The foundation promotes nonviolence, women's equality, and reproductive health—three things that Gloria herself has dedicated her life to.

In 1981, *Ms.* magazine scored another major victory when it was awarded the prestigious Peabody award for its HBO-produced show *She's Nobody's Baby: The History of American Women in the 20th Century*. This show, which was narrated by Alan Alda and Marlo Thomas, used music, cartoons, and newsreel footage to pay tribute to the women's liberation movement.

21. "Take Our Daughters to Work Day"— Helping Young Girls Challenge the Limits of What Is Possible

The impact of *Ms.* goes beyond the print format. One of its most significant contributions to the feminist movement was the inception of "Take Our Daughters to Work Day" in 1992. The Ms. Foundation for Women, which was started by the founding members of *Ms.* magazine to help create funding for feminist organizations throughout the world and was headed by Marie C. Wilson at the time, frequently collaborated with various artists and activists who were involved in the feminist cause one way or another.

Among them was Nell Merlino, an artist who acted as a consultant for the Ms. Foundation for Women at the time. While she was inspired by many things when deciding to create this special day for little girls in the US, her primary inspiration came from paying attention to the crowds in the subway that she observed in the morning and in the afternoon. In the morning, she would witness office-going crowds that were made up primarily of men, while in the afternoon, she would see a lot of school-going children—about half of whom were girls. This made her think about what was needed to make the morning crowd look more like the afternoon crowd in terms of gender representation.

At the time, second-wave feminism—spearheaded by Gloria—was already shining the spotlight on issues related to women in the workplace. This initiative aimed to target not only young girls but also their parents—helping them imagine a future where the girls' aspirations were given as much importance as the boys'. When Merlino and Wilson came up with the idea, they didn't have any idea how great of an impact it would end up having on young girls, their parents, and even the organizations that partnered with them to make this day possible.

Many people were involved in making this initiative a success, and one of them was Gloria Steinem. Gloria was on her way to meet *Parade* publisher Walter Anderson when she stopped at the foundation and learned about the proposal created by Merlino. Not only did she appreciate the idea but she wrote a piece for *Parade* and gave it to Anderson. The magazine enjoyed a wide circulation at the time and that small piece was instrumental in the foundation receiving almost 10,000 letters enquiring about this initiative from across the country. What was meant to be a pilot program in New York soon morphed into a national phenomenon that continues to the present day—only now it is known as "Take Our Daughters and Sons to Work Day."

Another heartwarming contribution made by Gloria to this initiative was that she made a small but significant change to the title. The original title—as envisioned by the team at Ms. Foundation—was "Take Your Daughters to Work Day." She suggested that they remove the "y" on "your" and make it "Take Our Daughters to Work Day," so that women who didn't have children would not feel excluded from the conversation. Thus, even as she focused on the popularization of feminist values and the empowerment of young women, she tried to be as inclusive and empathetic as possible.

22. Choice USA and the Fight for Reproductive Freedom

Gloria owed so many of her achievements—in fact, so much of her life—to the fact that she was able to exercise her reproductive choice when needed. She also understood that this was not an option that was available to many others at the time. As she became more closely involved with various movements across the country, she started to have some realizations. For one, she believed that the terms "pro-choice" and "pro-life" were misleading because they took the focus away from the main issue which was that the denial or restriction of abortion rights had always been about control.

She also understood that the health and happiness of women depended majorly on whether they had a say in matters related to their reproductive, menstrual, and even postnatal health. She has also famously said that if she is remembered in the future, it will be for coining the phrase "reproductive freedom."

It was her vision for a world where women will be able to experience reproductive freedom that inspired her to cofound "Choice USA" with Julie Burton and Kristina Kiehl in 1992. When it was first started, this organization helped provide support to the next generation of activists who were fighting for reproductive freedom at the time. In 2000, Choice USA decided to focus exclusively on youth. They participated in and led the youth contingent at the March for Women's Lives—a protest held to address topics related to women's rights and reproductive rights in 2004. The organization rebranded itself to "Unite for Gender and Reproductive Equity (URGE)" in 2014 as it broadened its objectives and became more inclusive.

Over the years, as women's reproductive freedoms have been threatened at both the state and national levels, Gloria has remained a vocal supporter and activist—lending her voice to various organizations that are fighting the good fight.

Chapter 4:

Politics and Feminism—Coming Into Her Own as an Activist and Organizer

All through her life, Gloria has lived with the understanding that the political is the personal and vice versa. She has been a part of many landmark political events in the country—as a journalist, as a volunteer, and as an activist and organizer. She has also been a part of various movements that brought women to the center of political life in the United States. As she turns 90, she still sees herself as an activist and organizer and urges the young people of this generation to exercise their right to have a say in the decisions that affect their lives.

23. Developing a Political Consciousness as a Young Girl

One of the first lessons Gloria learned about the overlap of personal and political issues was from her mother. Ruth was not only a well-read woman with a strong political consciousness of her own, but she also dreamed of being a journalist in New York one day. She understood the importance of staying informed and having open conversations regarding difficult topics. She shared her stories of depression with her daughter and also showed her how good political leadership could turn things around for a country.

Through her mother, Gloria also learned about the plight of Black people at the time and the trauma of those who were trapped in concentration camps in Europe. Thus, she understood how the people in power could affect the lives of ordinary people for better or worse. Her mother also helped her develop a sense of judgment when it came to choosing candidates and knowing which people and causes to support as she grew up. She learned to look beyond class, status, and money and only choose people based on their actions when deciding who was worth fighting for. Even as Gloria matured into her role as a lifelong protestor and activist, her mother's voice continued to guide her.

24. Anger and Frustration as a Politically Conscious Woman

As with many other things in her life, Gloria learned about the grim realities of life for women by observing her mother. Her mother had always deeply cared about various causes throughout her life, while at the same time being keenly aware of the fact that there was little she could do about it. Observing her mother made Gloria realize that a lot of what was identified as depression in her (and possibly other women) was simply anger turned inward.

As she became more politically conscious over time, she began to notice the same kind of anger within herself. She also understood why it was so difficult for her to express her anger and make peace with it in a healthy manner. As a woman, it was unacceptable for her to show anger, even as she understood the price she and other women paid for staying silent. This helped her understand that anger, for anger's sake, doesn't serve anyone, but anger turned into activism that can create a better world for everyone.

25. First Brush With Volunteering and Lessons Learned as a Woman Volunteer

When she was still in college, Gloria came across a campaigning center very close to the campus and decided to join it. The volunteers and campaigners worked to support Adlai Stevenson II's run for president. This was her first experience as a volunteer at a center like this and there were many things she loved about it. Most of all, she loved how it was open and accessible to everyone. In a way, it was her first brush with the power that otherwise ordinary individuals could wield by supporting and campaigning for the right candidates.

As much as she loved and learned from her experiences there, she also came to certain sobering truths as a woman in the field. For one, she came face-to-face with the discrimination made against both women and Black men who worked there. While White men were paid staff and made all the important decisions related to the campaign, women and Black men were volunteers or unpaid staffers, whose job it was to carry out the White men's orders.

While she was a volunteer, this was also her first "workplace" and this is where she realized how women at workplaces were tolerated at best and intimidated at worst. One such incident occurred when she and another volunteer were asked to stay out of Stevenson's sight when he visited the office because it was bad for his image to be seen by women who were not old enough to be his mother. This was because he was a divorcee, which made him vulnerable to judgment. Therefore, being seen with a younger woman could easily contribute to speculation about him having an affair, which could be extremely damaging to his reputation. What disgusted her most was the idea that a woman was responsible for both her and the man's behavior and that she had to adjust her life so that men were not inconvenienced or even tempted into bad behavior.

Despite these experiences, Gloria came away convinced that campaigns were all about hope, openness, and possibilities. This was a place where every vote mattered, which made her feel like every person mattered as well. While it would take her some more time to believe that she—and other women—could create change by wielding political power, she knew that she wanted to be a part of campaigns in the future.

26. Challenges Faced and Milestones Achieved in the First Stage of Her Political Journey

In her book *My Life on the Road* (Steinem, 2015), Gloria talks about the three stages of her political journey. In the first stage, she volunteered for campaigns much like the one in college. During this phase, she did everything from distributing leaflets to phone banking to doing research for campaigns. As a writer and journalist, she didn't get as many opportunities as she would have liked to talk about the issues that mattered to her. Here, too, she realized how easy it was to relegate female journalists to frivolous topics. For instance, when she wanted to cover a presidential candidate, she was asked to talk about his wife. However, she did get to be a part of the press corps for various campaigns, which gave her an opportunity to observe various presidential candidates, their styles and beliefs, and even their interactions with the press.

At the time, she wasn't directly involved in creating campaigns, but a high point on her journey was when, in 1972, she got a chance to write a televised speech for Shirley Chisholm—the first Black woman to be elected to the U.S. Congress. At the time, Shirley was running for the Democratic presidential election and needed a speech on short notice. Gloria was able to write it overnight and, in her own way, contribute to a historic event.

During this time, Gloria also came to a few realizations about herself. She understood that she might not do well as a politician—mostly because she preferred to avoid conflict as much as possible—but she could do really well as a volunteer. For one, she loved that volunteering was egalitarian in nature and that it allowed for the easy exchange of ideas. As an organizer, she recognized that she loved listening and creating solutions more than dealing with conflicts on a regular basis.

27. Experiences While Campaigning for Bella Azbug

One of the most meaningful relationships that Gloria formed as an activist and organizer was with Bella Azbug, a very important leader of second-wave feminism in the United States. Throughout her career, Bella donned several hats—that of a lawyer, politician, and activist. She also firmly believed in a harmonious relationship between nature and humans and was, thus, a prominent eco-feminist as well. When Gloria met Bella, she was struck by both her kindness and her political skills. At the time, Bella was running for Congress and Gloria was a part of her campaign.

On one hand, she saw how Bella concerned herself with real problems being faced by the country and its masses and threw her weight behind topics related to the civil rights movement, women's global peace movement, and nuclear testing. She was as involved in social activism as she was in mainstream politics. On the other hand, Gloria began to understand the pressures that women face in politics. Bella's working-class background made people take her less seriously, and her detractors believed that she didn't have a "motherly" image even though she was, in fact, a mother to two children.

Overall, however, working with Bella had its advantages. For starters, she didn't need to leave meetings because she was a woman in a room full of men, nor did she have to pass on her suggestions to men so that they would be taken seriously. Most importantly, she was able to assess Bella's impact simply by walking with her through the streets of New York and interacting with her supporters who came from all walks of life. Bella was elected to Congress in 1970, and their relationship set the stage for many important collaborations throughout their lives.

28. Formation of the National Women's Political Caucus—Bringing Women to the Center of Politics

The second stage of Gloria's activism career came into being in 1971 when she became part of the National Women's Political Caucus (NWPC). This organization—which was to create history on many fronts for the women's movement—was created when three Congresswomen decided that they needed more pro-equality women in both elected and appointed offices. These women were Shirley, Bella, and Patsy Mink—who was the first Asian-American woman elected to Congress. These women understood the importance of diversity in politics, and they also acknowledged the need for women to rise above party lines for this cause.

Gloria was part of a 24-member committee made up of women who came from diverse fields. The aim of NWPC was to combat racism, sexism, institutional violence, and poverty while ensuring that more women were elected or appointed to positions of power. The members were asked to either meet the caucuses that had already been formed or to create new caucuses at the city and state levels. Gloria was also chosen to talk to the media as the spokesperson for the Democratic convention and inform them of any relevant developments at the NWPC.

The organization was a success on multiple fronts. Their goal was to get 50% of delegates from both parties combined elected, and they also wanted greater diversity among them. They also emphasized that all these delegates needed to have reproductive freedom as a part of their manifesto. While they fell short of the 50% target, they were able to achieve a little more than 33%, which was an all-time record.

While they could not make "reproductive freedom" a reality at the time, it was the first time that a major party had voted on the topic, which was a win in itself. While Shirley's presence brought attention to the NWPC, the movement was also credited for increasing people's trust in politicians in general. Over the years, NWPC has been instrumental in creating an environment where women's issues are no longer pushed to the background. It has also helped women understand that they needed to be the change they were seeking in the world.

29. Formation of the Women's Action Alliance— Empowering Grassroots Feminism

Gloria's experiences as a feminist organizer proved to her that all movements begin at the grassroots level. Her experiences in India helped her recognize that she needed to talk to both men and women in order to understand the challenges faced by the feminist movement at the local level. Gloria also understood that the grassroots feminist movement cannot be seen as something homogenous, much like feminists themselves could not be grouped together all the time. Therefore, she—along with Catherine Samuels, Brenda Feigen-Fasteau, and others—started the Women's Action Alliance (WAA) in 1971.

The WAA had two main goals: one, to document the different tactics used by local feminist organizations and understand their similarities and differences, and two, to bring about change at the grassroots level by engaging with various stakeholders. Gloria believed that women needed access to relevant information and resources to change their lives. She also wanted to design programs that allowed women to come together irrespective of their race, class, and age.

The impact of the WAA was immense. For one, its observations related to the various feminist organizations showed a remarkable similarity in their techniques—even if they were separated by geography, ideology, and specific aims. Also, the WAA was perhaps the first organization that documented the workings of these local organizations. These documents help scholars and feminists alike to understand how grassroots feminist organizations really worked, as well as to learn from the best practices they employed during that period.

Another achievement of the WAA was the considerable amount of correspondence they received from men and women alike—trying to understand their work, access important information, and also seek advice where needed. In fact, within a few months of its formation, the organization was receiving almost 200 letters each week. These letters then prompted the leaders to start various programs at the local level. For instance, they were able to talk to parents and teachers about avoiding sexism in the curricula for students, and even help them learn nonsexist child-rearing techniques. In many cases, they encouraged women to explore nontraditional occupations.

They also helped reduce the instances of substance abuse among women and help school girls to use computers to their advantage. Even though the WAA had to be dissolved in 1997 because they were unable to secure enough funding to continue, they created a positive impact at the grassroots level—something that was difficult even for national and state-level organizations to achieve at the time.

30. Campaigning for the Equal Rights Amendment

Perhaps one of the most important political struggles of Gloria's life was campaigning for the Equal Rights Amendment (ERA) through the National Organization for Women (NOW) and the NWPC. At the time that ERA was introduced in Congress in 1923, women had only been voting for three years in the United States. The underlying basis of the ERA was that neither the country nor any of the states could make laws that discriminated against women on the basis of gender. It also gave Congress the right to enforce these amendments to the U.S. Constitution.

The detractors of the ERA mainly believed that it would take away a lot of protections and exemptions that women enjoyed on account of their gender. Second-wave feminists and supporters of the ERA, however, believed that gender-discriminatory laws often kept women in a state of economic dependence and took away their agency in relationships. They believed that laws related to job opportunities and child support, for instance, could not be limited to only one gender.

Gloria joined many other feminists on various protests and panels to put pressure on Congress. Ultimately, the Senate approved the ERA in March 1972. Interestingly, it was not ratified by the required majority of the states until 2020 and it still isn't included as a part of the U.S. Constitution, much to Gloria's shock. Nevertheless, she played a very crucial role in getting the ERA approved. In 1970, she published a brilliant essay in *TIME* called "What Would It Be Like if Women Win" (Steinem, 1970).

In this brilliant essay, she took on the many criticisms that the ERA and the Women's Liberation Movement faced—specifically that these laws and changes were threatening or destroying the American family. For one, she compared the state of U.S. politics to that of countries like India and Sweden where women were already ruling the country or where both partners took equal responsibility in child-rearing. Also, she argued that giving women the option to pursue equal opportunities in the workplace does not mean that women who wanted to be homemakers or focus entirely on being stay-at-home moms could not do so. These opportunities were possibilities for those who were looking for more in their lives but didn't have the means to do so.

She also argued that when the gender roles weren't as rigid as they were then, it would help both men and women become more than cliched stereotypes as partners and parents. In many senses, this would help them become true partners, thus strengthening their relationship over time. Also, these laws would help those whose identities and lifestyles did not fit the heteronormative mold. It would liberate the terms "marriage" and "family" from their rigid definitions and create a more inclusive and healthier world.

Last but not least, she also argued that approval of the ERA would not just be a big win for the Women's Liberation Movement, but also lead to men's liberation by creating an environment where they can talk openly about their mental health struggles, share their financial burdens with their partner, and avoid toxic notions of "masculinity." This way, it would help them improve their mental and physical health and maybe even increase their longevity by improving their quality of life.

She ended the essay by saying that "the most radical goal of the movement is egalitarianism." In 1970, Gloria also testified before the Senate and made a speech that explained why the ERA was important for the women of the United States.

31. Gloria's Views on Equal Voting Rights and the Importance of Voting

Gloria is the granddaughter of a woman who was a prominent figure in the suffrage movement and has always held very strong views on the importance of voting for everyone, but especially for women. Having been a part of various elections, Gloria understood the difference that even a few votes could make and the effect that a candidate's victory could have on various aspects of the country's governance. She knew how various powerful people were connected to each other, how one candidate could choose other candidates and lobby for them in order to further their agenda, and how these decisions could then become the basis for either reform or regression.

She believes that "voting isn't the most we can do but it is the least" (Steinem, 2015). She believes that the voting booth is the one place in the world where the least powerful has as much influence as the most powerful and that the right to vote is, in many ways, the right to exist.

While actively working on campaigns, she realized that when women didn't just support campaigns or movements, but instead created campaigns based on the issues that mattered to them, they were better able to effect change. It also became clear to her that women were much more likely to vote on issues like family planning and health, education, violence, and equality. This is simply because these issues disproportionately affect women, which is why it's even more important that women fight for their right to vote at all times.

These issues are not limited to only women, though. Anyone who identifies as being a part of a marginalized group also faces the danger of voter suppression tactics—such as limits to early voting, issues with photo IDs, and even restricted access to voting in some cases. The thing is, if these people are able to exercise their right to vote, they will also be able to make decisions that improve their lives. Over the years, Gloria has publicly advocated for the right to vote, and has, time and again, urged people to cast their votes.

Chapter 5:

Travels Around the World and the Impact on Her Work— Recontextualizing Feminism in Different Cultural Settings

Just like her father, Gloria has the heart of a traveler. Even though, as a child, she often wished for "stability" and conventionality, she soon realized that she enjoyed traveling. In fact, when she first visited India after graduating from Smith, she learned so much about grassroots organization, cooperation, and listening to people about their problems that she incorporated them as part of her work in later years. Through the years, she has traveled all over the world and had numerous experiences that helped her become a better feminist and a better human being.

32. Gloria's Travels in India and Her Relationship With the Country

It took Gloria 20 years to come back to the country where she had first learned the lessons of grassroots organization and Gandhian principles. During her first visit, she met Devaki Jain, a renowned Indian economist who has worked in the fields of social justice and women empowerment. Devaki was also a believer in Gandhian principles and wanted Gloria to come back to India and engage in conversations with the women's groups she was working with at the time. This was in the 1970s, by which time Gloria had already become a part of various feminist organizations and rallies and knew a thing or two about creating a feminist revolution at the local and national levels.

One of the most impactful lessons that Gloria learned during her first stint in India was the use of nonviolent resistance to protest against any form of suppression. Not only that, but she thought that the idea of boycotting consumer products in order to put pressure on oppressing systems was especially well-suited to women's protests. By this time, she was also documenting the various tactics used by feminist grassroots movements in the United States, and she—along with Devaki—decided to do something similar in India.

As they were preparing a pamphlet full of Gandhian tactics for women to use in India, they met Kamladevi Chattopadhyay. Kamladevi Chattopadhyay was a visionary and a very important part of India's independence struggle. Not only was she the first Indian woman to stand for elections post-independence, but she was also responsible for the revival of Indian arts, handicrafts, and theater in independent India. She had worked very closely with Gandhi during the independence struggle and had led his women's organization at the time.

She told Gloria and Devaki how Gandhi had leaned heavily on her and the women's organization during the freedom struggle, which made Gloria realize that, once again, an entire movement was credited to men without paying attention to the women who made it possible. Also, by this time, Gloria had worked so closely with feminist grassroots organizations throughout the US that she couldn't help but notice the similarities between them and the village movements in India. Once again, she was convinced that these movements were linked in their own ways. Gloria has since returned to India numerous times and her bond with the country has remained strong as ever.

33. Apne Aap Worldwide and Her Work Related to It

Over the years, another Indian woman has become a trusted friend and collaborator to Gloria. Ruchira Gupta, who is a writer, professor, and feminist activist, is the founder of Apne Aap Worldwide, a nongovernmental organization that works to eradicate sex trafficking and also promotes female empowerment. The organization came into being when 22 women belonging to a red-light district in Mumbai became part of *The Selling of Innocents*—an award-winning documentary by Ruchira Gupta in 1996.

These 22 women knew what it meant to be treated as objects and to be afforded very little dignity and even less opportunity to better their condition. They decided to meet each other in parks and derived strength from each other. Collectively, they felt seen, heard, and empowered and believed, maybe for the first time, that they could imagine a different future for themselves. In 2002, the organization came into being in Mumbai.

In the last couple of decades, Ruchira has been joined by Gloria in their shared quest to improve the lives of trafficked and prostituted women and also to end intergenerational prostitution among tribes in Delhi, Haryana, Rajasthan, West Bengal, and Bihar. Gloria has visited India quite a few times in order to interact with women in these areas and to create awareness among them and among those working to help them imagine better lives. Her work has also helped her notice the similarities between the conditions of women who are trafficked for sex as well as the people and systems who create and perpetuate the conditions for it. Interestingly, Ruchira also edited Gloria's 2014 book, *As if Women Matter.*

34. Lessons Learned Regarding Sex Work and the True Emancipation of Women

Having traveled all over the world and having been a part of various "talking circles," Gloria has been able to understand both the plight and the power of women in various cultures. For one, these travels have helped her move beyond stereotypes that are otherwise prevalent among those who are privileged and aren't aware of the realities of sex work. Second, she has witnessed similar issues and similar systems of oppression among women, whether they are from India or the US, Zambia or Amsterdam. Not only has she traveled extensively for conferences on sex trafficking all across the world but she has also spent time talking to the women who are directly affected by it.

During one of these talking circles in Zambia, she realized that some women had to take up prostitution because they didn't have enough money to build an electric fence to keep the elephants out. Without this fence, their crops would get badly damaged and they would suffer economically because of it. This isn't something that would be obvious without building trust with these women and understanding the real problems behind their condition.

When Gloria was able to raise funds for these women, the women were able to grow crops and earn enough money to ensure school fees for their children and food security for the upcoming year. Talking to young girls in tribal communities in India, where they are groomed to join the sex trade at a very young age, Gloria was surprised to find their spirit and courage intact. She also witnessed how the young girls and women were more than eager to help each other out and all they needed was someone who listened to them.

Finally, her awareness of various cultures in the world also helped her understand that the usual measures to curb the sex trade were not really helpful, at least not to the women trapped in it. She gives the example of various Nordic countries where, instead of the sex trade being legalized or criminalized (the two models that most countries follow), the situation is handled differently. In those countries, sex workers are not penalized or arrested; in fact, they are given healthcare and other necessary services and are also helped with understanding the various alternatives available to them. On the other hand, those who traffic these women or who promote the sex trade are punished severely for their actions. This way, punishment is given to those who rob others of their bodily autonomy and not to the women whose autonomy has been robbed or who are exercising their autonomy while participating in sex work.

35. Life on the Road—A Lifetime of Lessons

Throughout her life, Gloria has seen the road as a constant companion as well as a teacher. Ever since she was a child, she learned a lot about herself and others on the road. So much so, that she decided to write about these diverse, sometimes challenging but always enthralling experiences in her memoir *Life on the Road*. Through her travels, she came again and again to the conclusion that her experiences in one part of the world would be corroborated in another part of the world that had seemingly no connection to the first. She was so used to living out of a suitcase, so to speak, that at one point, she realized that the longest she had been home at one time was eight days.

Travel has also been an important part of her feminist campaigning and organizing life. In fact, she was introduced to the third stage of campaigning in her sixties. During this time, she gathered her closest activist friends in a van and traveled across the United States to effect change in "swing states." She found that women in the swing states could change the course of elections, but also that certain women—especially those who supported the Republicans—felt isolated and misunderstood by many of the mainstream feminist political groups. Even though these were extremely important states, Gloria found that very few activists, politicians, or even media persons went there and worked at the local level.

When Gloria and her friends stayed in these places and talked to the women about their needs and concerns, they realized that many of them were amenable to change. At the very least, they were willing to listen simply because they were being listened to. In states such as Colorado, for example, these efforts changed the course of history and helped elect candidates who cared about the health and happiness of women and minorities.

36. A Traveler Who Doesn't Drive?

Since Gloria had seen firsthand what a lifetime of travel had done to her mother, Gloria wanted to learn to drive when she was younger. She saw it as an act of asserting her independence and even applied for a driver's ed course. However, by the time she returned from her first visit to India, she had spent so much time on trains, buses, and other means of communal travel that she began to understand its numerous benefits. As a feminist who was still finding her way in the world, she realized that she could learn a lot simply by listening to people— especially women—talk to each other and to her on these modes of public transport.

She also recognized that if she was always driving, she would not be able to have in-depth conversations with others, nor would she be able to meet new people in the isolation of her car. Therefore, she decided to travel in taxis for the rest of her life and has learned a lot from the many taxi drivers she has met on the road. She has been able to immerse herself in the taxi drivers' worlds and exchange stories with them. In the process, she learned a lot as a writer, organizer, and human being. For one, she could see that many taxi drivers had a better sense of politics, society, and culture than many pundits. This is because they were always conversing with others on the road and they were often either immigrants or closely working with them. In other words, if there was a change happening in the country, they would likely be able to predict it better than most others.

While she has met her fair share of extremists and strange people in taxis, she has met far more amazing people who taught her something or reaffirmed her faith in the work she was doing. In fact, the quote that is frequently associated with Gloria—"Honey, if men could become pregnant, abortion would be a sacrament" (Brockes, 2015)—

was something that an Irish female cab driver told her and her partner Florynce Kennedy at one time. Similarly, an encounter with a very young cabbie taught Gloria the importance of truly seeing with her own eyes rather than seeing the world as she was instructed by others. Another female driver told her that her feminist work had helped even loners like her, which Gloria took as high praise.

Many of these taxi drivers reminded Gloria of her father and his reasons for traveling as a way of staying independent in body and spirit. Another amazing experience that Gloria had when she was in Brooklyn was the discovery of Black Pearl, a taxi service started by Calvin Williams—an African American man who later served two terms in the New York State Assembly. Black Pearl was started as an answer to the yellow cabs whose drivers often did not go to the Black neighborhoods and its motto was "We're Not Yellow, We'll Go Anywhere." Talking to these taxi drivers helped her see how even a mode of transport could become a means of creating a new future full of possibilities.

37. Travel to North Korea and the Work of a "Citizen Diplomat"

In a historical event, Gloria, along with 30 other women who were also peace activists, traveled to North Korea on May 24, 2015, and crossed the demilitarized zone—a heavily fortified border between South Korea and North Korea. This day was not chosen by accident. It is known as International Women's Day for Peace and Disarmament, and women activists from all over the world chose this day to foster peace and harmony between the two nations.

After crossing the zone, the activists held a symposium with North Korean women's groups in Pyongyang in a bid to improve the relations between the countries. According to Gloria, the act of walking through the demilitarized zone was of huge significance because it was the first time that something like this had been successfully attempted. She also emphasized that the trip was an important step toward peace and reconciliation between the two countries and that the group of women were able to act as citizen diplomats in this case. Gloria has called that day, the day she crossed the demilitarized zone with other feminists, the longest day of her life in every way.

38. Learning About Dignity and Freedom From Flight Attendants

As much as Gloria has traveled by road, she has also taken countless flights across the world because of her writing and speaking engagements and even her work as a feminist organizer and activist. Even though she would often be too exhausted to interact with flight attendants, she slowly started developing friendships with many of them and learning about the challenges they faced in their profession. She learned that the first female flight attendants were actually registered nurses who were trained in various emergency procedures. Even after that, an average flight attendant needed to be well-trained in safety and evacuation procedures, rescue skills, precautions against hijacking, and various other life-saving skills. However, they were "valued" only for their height, weight, and age in the industry, and they were often overworked and devalued at the same time.

Not only did they have to deal with sexism and harassment from many of the male customers, but they could be penalized and even fired for trying to raise their voices against mistreatment. They had to follow strict rules like not dating or marrying someone while they were employed, were paid much less than pilots, and were treated poorly as well. The worst part, perhaps, was the industry itself discriminated against women and objectified them in order to attract rich male customers.

During her travels, however, Gloria also witnessed closely how these flight attendants remained calm and empathetic even though they weren't always treated well themselves. Not only that, but she also became aware of little acts of resistance that these women engaged in on a regular basis. For example, as much as they campaigned for greater salaries and more workplace safety, they also demanded that they be addressed by their full names or surnames instead of their first names. Later, perhaps inspired by *Ms.*, many asked to be identified as such so that their marital status would not have any bearing on their job.

In the mid-1970s, Gloria visited a group called "Stewardesses for Women's Rights" in the Rockefeller Center, where she saw women take part in unions to demand better pay, protest against discriminatory and degrading practices (like being objectified in advertisements), and also exposing certain unsafe practices followed by various airlines. She addressed the first national conference for the Stewardesses for Women's Rights in 1973 and continued to support them for the entire duration of their existence.

39. Gloria's Advice Regarding the Importance of Travel

As someone who has seen both the benefits and struggles that come with constant travel, Gloria is in a great position to talk about the importance of travel. Even today, she tries to travel as much as she can, not only to educate others but also herself. Interestingly, Gloria has never been able to keep a journal while on the road, as the intensity of travel keeps her from making note of the numerous stories that become a part of her life. So, she usually compiles these stories when she is at home and then gives herself to the road for the rest of the year.

She encourages anyone who can travel to do so as much as possible, even those who cannot or don't want to physically travel because it helps to foster the mentality of a traveler. According to Gloria, travel is what helps us get "out of denial and into reality" (Steinem, 2015). Additionally, it helps us experience things instead of simply thinking or talking about them, and it helps us overcome our fears and take action where needed. According to Gloria, "It's right up there with life-threatening emergencies and truly mutual sex as a way of being fully alive in the present" (Steinem, 2015).

Chapter 6:

Gloria Steinem and Intersectionality—Using Her Voice to Champion Various Interlinked Causes

Gloria realized early on in life that we can only be free when everyone is free. In other words, feminism could not be a real success until it also recognized and made space for other struggles—such as those of people of color or the working class. As she grew in fame and stature, she used her ability to talk to people and her love for travel to understand the issues that face marginalized communities in the US as well as across the world. Time after time, she came up against the realization that people created hierarchies as a way to keep people divided and wary of each other. In the 1970s, there wasn't enough discussion or awareness around "intersectional feminism," even though many, many Black and working-class feminists tried to talk about it. Over the years, however, many feminists—including Gloria—have begun to see intersectionality as a core tenet of feminism.

40. Feminism and the Civil Rights Movement

When Gloria was still a freelance journalist in 1963—and had not yet become the feminist leader and organizer that we know today—she got to know about Martin Luther King, Jr.'s march in Washington, D.C., and wanted to cover it. At the time, she could hardly get any political pieces assigned to her, and though she got an opportunity to write about James Baldwin—who was both a famous writer and a well-regarded civil rights activist—she wasn't sure if following him around at the march would be a good idea. There were also concerns about safety at the march, so she almost didn't go. As it turned out, the march was both a historic event for her to witness and a lesson in the intersection of feminism as well as Black power that she remembered for the rest of her life.

At the march, she met a woman named Mrs. Greene, who had come with her daughter, who talked to her about the absence of women in these movements. She made her realize that women were not allowed to address the gathering even at such marches and that women who had sacrificed a lot while protesting for their rights were not talked about as much as they should. She showed Gloria how the issues of race, social class, and gender were interconnected rather than disparate, and took the time to teach her that White women needed to first stand up for themselves before they could stand up for others. This was perhaps one of the earliest times that Gloria was reminded of the need for intersectionality in the feminist movement and also that feminism needed people of color as much as they needed feminism.

41. A Woman Nudges History Into Existence

The march that was held on August 28, 1963, was historic for numerous reasons, but perhaps none more than the speech given by Martin Luther King, Jr. Isn't it amazing that the most famous part of the speech, the one the speech is remembered by—"I have a dream"—

was not even a part of King's original speech. Believe it or not, we have a woman to thank for that.

Mahalia Jackson was a legendary gospel singer who often introduced Martin's speech to the crowds. On that day, he asked Mahalia to open his speech with a classic gospel song called "I've Been 'Buked, and I've Been Scorned." Since the two of them worked so closely with each other, they knew each other's work intimately as well. When Martin began his speech, Mahalia perhaps felt that it could be taken in a daring new direction. She had heard him deliver similar speeches in the past and knew about the major themes that he touched upon. Therefore, in a pivotal moment, she said out loud to him, "Tell them about the dream, Martin" (Mullen, 2022). Upon hearing this, Martin put aside his prepared notes and began his history-making speech. Gloria witnessed how the presence—and presence of mind—of a woman helped create history at that march.

42. Protests Against Apartheid in 1984

In December of 1984, Gloria joined around 150 people in protest against the South African government's practice of apartheid. These protests were being held in Washington, D.C. as a part of the "Free South Africa" movement by the group known as TransAfrica. During this peaceful march held outside the South African embassy, Gloria was arrested along with two other protestors.

At the time, Gloria criticized the South African government for denying basic human and civil rights to its majority Black population. Since she was known as a feminist, she also highlighted the reason behind campaigning for Black rights by saying that she opposed any and all systems of caste as they usually discriminated against women.

43. The Connection Between Women's Rights, Democracy, and Peace

Time and again, Gloria has highlighted the connection between women's rights and peace in the world. According to her, the single biggest determinant of whether a country is violent toward others is whether it is violent toward women. She has talked about how women are in constant danger for their lives all around the world. In some places, this happens because they are discriminated against at birth—leading to female infanticide. In other cases, they have to contend with female genital mutilation, rapes, domestic violence, honor killings, sex trafficking, and so on. She also talks about how sex trafficking today is almost as big of an industry as the arms and drugs trade. While some parts of the world might engage in one kind of violence, others might engage in something else.

In a 2016 United Nations address, she urged the delegates to stop thinking of these issues as either women's issues or even children's issues and instead think of them as world issues. She also asked them to look at a country's treatment of its women if they wanted to understand whether it was truly peaceful and democratic and to include women's empowerment and liberation as a crucial part of their foreign policy agendas.

44. Gloria's Views on President Bush and His War Policies

Throughout her life, Gloria has witnessed and reported on so many politicians in action that she has a firm grasp on their policies as well as the intentions behind those policies. She was a vocal critic of President George W. Bush's policies, especially those related to the Gulf War in 1990 and 1991, and another war against Iraq and Afghanistan after the 9/11 attacks. She has always believed that no matter what his purported agenda, Bush targeted Iraq because he was after their rich oil reserves.

In 1991, toward the end of the war, Gloria—along with feminists Kate Millett and Robin Morgan—signed a letter to the editor of the *New York Times*, denouncing the war and calling out the government for pretending that the war was about defending democracy in the Middle East.

In the letter titled "We Learned the Wrong Lessons in Vietnam; A Feminist Issue Still," Gloria called out the hypocrisy of the U.S. government of the time, reminding them that they could not pretend to fight Saddam Hussein as they were when previously they had armed him so that he could massacre the Kurds using chemical warfare. She pointed out that, as feminists, they couldn't forget Vietnam and were opposed to the war in the Persian Gulf. Most importantly, she talked about how the war could not possibly have protected democracy in the Middle Eastern countries, as people had no voting rights in Saudi Arabia, women were not allowed to drive cars, and women were not allowed to vote in Kuwait. Not only that, but homosexuals were also executed in those countries, meaning no one's rights were truly being protected. Throughout her life, Gloria has called war "a feminist issue" (Millett et al., 1991) and used it as a measure to uncover a particular politician's or government's true agenda.

45. Feminism Against War and Human Rights Violations

After the 9/11 attacks, there was understandable fear and grief among the people of New York as well as the entire United States. However, antiwar activists, social workers, and feminist groups already sensed that this attack—and the anger and grief of the public—would be used to declare war on Afghanistan, Iraq, and possibly other Middle Eastern countries. They also knew, from experience, that these measures would do nothing to either alleviate the risk of terrorism or to change the condition of people in the targeted countries. If anything, it would make things much, much worse.

When Gloria took a cab after the 9/11 attacks, she could see anonymous graffiti on walls all over New York that said, "Our grief is not a cry for war" (Steinem, 2015). Her cab driver agreed and told her that this was how most people in New York felt. Since they knew exactly how it felt to be attacked, they didn't want to do the same to another country. Gloria joined many distinguished people—like civil rights veteran Rosa Parks and intellectual Edward Said—in supporting these antiwar cries by signing the Justice, not Revenge petition started by members of the Institute for Policy Studies.

While Gloria has been critical of Bush for a long time, she also sensed that the tide was turning. She realized that the people were becoming aware of his agendas, and they were also becoming aware of what people in other countries thought about his policies. Most importantly, she was hopeful about the fact that public opinion against his War on Terror had been formed much faster than their opinion against the Vietnam War in the past. So, while a lot still needed to be done, there was hope for an antiwar future.

46. Gloria and the Women's Rights Movements in Afghanistan

In 2001, Gloria started working closely with various feminist groups both in the US and in Afghanistan to help restore the rights they had lost after the Taliban's takeover of the country. In a conversation with CNN, she talked about the various ways in which feminist groups, as well as aid organizations, could help these women empower themselves. For one, she urged everyone in power to listen to the women themselves and to pay attention to what they truly needed. She also asked the government to stop spending money on arms or providing arms to the militants and to instead focus on providing emergency aid directly to the NGOs in Afghanistan.

She has worked closely with members of the Revolutionary Association of Women of Afghanistan (RAWA) and many other feminist organizations in the country. She believes that the US could play a huge role in improving women's conditions simply by disarming their oppressors. She has also expressed her faith in the many Afghan women leaders she has met over the years.

47. Acknowledging the Role of Religion in the Suppression of Women's Rights

Gloria grew up proud of her Jewish heritage and also understood how religion could be used as a way to control women's autonomy. In India, she saw how the caste system was used not only to strip women who were in the lower caste of their basic human rights but also to control and subjugate women of higher casts. Similarly, as part of her fight for reproductive freedom for women in the United States, Gloria has also witnessed how Christofascist leaders used religion to deter women from accessing abortion and contraception.

She has always been a part of events where religious impositions on women were challenged and where women could participate fully in the customs and traditions that they wanted to. In fact, she has urged that we move on from a focus on religion to one on spirituality, as it allows women to reclaim their stories and connect with the divine in ways that don't threaten their autonomy.

At the same time, Gloria doesn't stand for disrespect to other religions under the pretext of feminism. The same goes for the flak that certain countries in the Global South receive for their treatment of women without calling attention to the atrocities that occur in their home country. In fact, her travels have helped her see how some countries might be ahead of the US in some aspects, while still lagging behind in others. She condemns and resists Islamophobia, which is often masked as concern for women's rights in the Middle East and other Muslim-majority countries. When asked about her beliefs regarding the role of Islam in suppressing women's rights, she maintains that it does not play a greater role than, say, Christianity, Hinduism, or even Buddhism "when they are imposed as totalitarian systems" (*Gloria Steinem: Restoring Women's Rights in Afghanistan*, 2001).

48. Participating in Feminist Seders in Manhattan

In 1976, Esther M. Broner—a Jewish feminist writer and activist— published a feminist Haggadah in *Ms.* magazine. The Haggadah is a text containing the story of the Exodus and setting the order for the Passover seder. Esther and other Jewish feminists like Gloria realized that women were excluded from many rituals of the seder and were also sidelined when it came to the stories that were told during the seder. The book, titled *A Stolen Legacy, A Women's Haggadah* talks about the "exodus of women" (Brozan, 1990). The Haggadah is often seen as a text that allows for the telling and retelling of the stories of Jews, especially those who, traditionally, have not been given a voice in the original stories. In *A Woman's Haggadah*, the stories and voices of women have been given the importance they deserve.

Since women who were involved in and passionate about their religion felt like outsiders in their own religious groups, they decided to reclaim their narrative by participating in feminist Passover Seders. The first such seder was held at Esther's apartment in Manhattan in 1976 and became a yearly tradition after that. The group of feminist leaders who started this tradition and who participated in it for years called themselves the "seder sisters." Apart from Esther, this group contained regulars like Bella Azbug, Gloria, and writer Grace Paley—who have been referred to as the group's spiritual leaders.

Over time, these feminist seders became mainstream, and more and more women began to look for "egalitarian" Haggadah and tried to form their own groups where they could create traditions and stories to pass on to their daughters. In a way, the objective of the first feminist seder was fulfilled.

49. Gloria on the Intersection of Gender and Labor

Just as race plays an important role in the fight for women's liberation, so too does labor. Gloria has always been concerned about how women's work is valued both at home and in the outside world. Growing up, she had seen her mother buckle under the weight of managing a home, taking care of her two daughters, and dealing with her husband's whimsical business ideas and his penchant for frequent travel. She saw how all of that labor went unnoticed. As an adult, she saw even more clearly how women's work was devalued by various industries.

In her 1994 book *Moving Beyond Words* (Steinem, 1994), she wrote an essay called "Revaluing Economics." In the essay, she argued that labor wasn't always recognized or rewarded according to the expertise required for a certain kind of job or even according to the demands of the market, but according to the social status of the person doing the job. This means that, in general, a job becomes highly valued if elite White men do it, loses some of its value when men of color or working-class men do it, and terribly devalued if women do it. She pointed out that as soon as women begin to enter an industry in larger numbers, men either try to exit it or create unnecessary distinctions between their roles and those of women. All of this has a very real economic impact on women and minorities.

It was her understanding of the ill effects of labor discrimination on the basis of gender that encouraged her to support the creation of organizations that helped ease the divide in various industries. One such organization—that came into being in 1974—was the Coalition of Labor Union Women (CLUW). Gloria Steinem was one of the founding members of this organization, which created when representatives of 58 feminist trade unions came together In Chicago.

The initial conference was attended by almost 3,000 women. The broad objectives of the organization were to help pass laws that were favorable to women workers—especially in terms of health care and equal pay, to encourage more women to join unions and participate in union activities, and push for the eradication of policies that discriminated on the basis of gender. Not only that, but the CLUW aimed to implement parental leave and childcare policies that would allow women to participate as equal partners both at work and at home.

Many local chapters of CLUW fought to include abortion and contraception access as part of the contract for their workers and supported the ERA—thus proving that true feminism could not exist without fair labor laws.

50. Frontline Women's Fund—Empowering Activists Across the Globe

Having worked closely with feminist grassroots organizations in India, the US, and other parts of the world, and having witnessed the challenges faced by these organizations, Gloria understood the importance of providing financial aid to women activists all over the world. In 2011, she cofounded the Frontline Women's Fund, along with lawyer and human rights activist Jessica Neuwirth and UN High Commissioner for Human Rights Navi Pillay.

They understood that while frontline feminist organizations around the world played an extremely crucial role in promoting equality and safeguarding women's rights, they had limited access to funds. Not only that, but only one percent of funding for gender equality actually went to women's organizations and even less went to frontline groups. This is the gap that Gloria and her team wanted to bridge when they started the fund, then known as Donor Direct Action.

In 2015, this organization became a part of the Sisterhood Is Global Institute, a feminist organization founded by Simone de Beauvoir and Robin Morgan in 1984. The impact of the organization has been immense. For one, it has helped increase the access of frontline feminist workers to both media and political resources. It has also helped regrant almost $6 million to frontline organizations across the world. One of these frontline organizations supported by the Sisterhood Is Global Institute is the Gloria Steinem Equality Fund, which aims to end sex trafficking and works with 13 grantees worldwide.

51. Gloria's Support for Queer Rights as a Feminist

Feminism, especially in its earlier forms, often faced criticisms around inclusiveness. One of the most common forms of criticism was that most feminists were not supporters of queer rights. In fact, the feminist Betty Friedan—who was also the leader of the National Organization for Women (NOW)—used the term "lavender menace" in a 1969 meeting to denote how the presence of lesbians in the women's liberation movement detracted from its overall goals. While there were many lesbians who supported LGBTQ+ rights at the time, there were those who shared Betty's beliefs about them. This alienated many lesbians from the movement and even gave rise to the group known as "The Lavender Menace" in 1970. Though NOW included lesbian rights among its policies in 1970, and even Betty apologized to them in 1977, a lot of damage had been done to the credibility of the movement by then.

In almost direct contrast to this, Gloria has always been a vocal supporter of queer rights—especially lesbian rights—and has tried to include them in the mainstream movement as much as possible. In 1972, when *Ms.* magazine printed its first official issue, it included an article called "Can Women Love Women?" thus centering lesbian love in the feminist magazine. Over the years, *Ms.* established itself as a safe space for lesbians to talk about their experiences and explore their own feelings about their sexual identity.

One of these people was Claudia Stallman, who had written a letter to *Ms.* when she was 16 years old that talked about the conflicting feelings she experienced regarding her homosexuality. She also talked about the need to protect herself from the realities of society at the time. In 2018, Claudia was the project director for the Lesbian and Gay Family Building Project at Binghamton University and she got an opportunity to read that letter aloud once more. She believed that *Ms.* had made space in the world for young girls and women like her.

When Kate Millett, who was closely connected to the feminist movement, came out as bisexual, the information was used by mainstream media like *TIME* to undermine the feminist movement. In fact, the piece—entitled "Women's Lib: A Second Look"—talked about how this would discredit the movement by enforcing the belief that all feminists are lesbians (that they only choose feminism because they don't like men or don't want to be with them).

This enraged Gloria and her allies and urged them to release a statement of solidarity with homosexuals, stating that both lesbianism and women's liberation are about women's autonomy, and hence they supported both equally. Gloria has always maintained that both queer people and straight women have the same enemies and, therefore, they could never be separated from each other. For many people who came to terms with their sexual identity at the time, Gloria was one of the few feminists who helped them feel accepted by the movement.

52. Gloria's Views on the Kinsey Report

In 1953, Alfred Kinsey—a sexologist and biologist who founded the Kinsey Institute for Research in Sex, Gender, and Reproduction—published a landmark book called *Sexual Behavior in the Human Female*. Though he published a book called *Sexual Behavior in the Human Male* in 1948, this book was exceptional because it was the first time such a detailed analysis had been done of women's sexual behavior in the United States. In the book, he discussed issues that had never been discussed publicly before—especially those regarding adultery and premarital sex. While there have been legitimate concerns about some of the mistakes in his methodologies, it's widely believed that this book is important for many reasons.

On the 50th anniversary of this book's publication, Indiana University celebrated his life and work all year long. Gloria Steinem was invited to deliver a lecture on Kinsey and the evolution of female sexuality at the time. Gloria celebrated the fact that he dedicated a large part of his research to understanding women's sexuality, the first and perhaps, even today, the most comprehensive of its kind. She acknowledged its imperfections but also saw it as a huge step forward in signaling the beginning of the end of the repression of women's sexuality. She also urged that the "Kinsey reports"—as these books are called—need to be accessed and utilized for their influence to prevail.

Chapter 7:

Controversies and Challenges That Have Shaped Her Life

For decades, Gloria Steinem has been known as the "world's most famous feminist." The acclaim has helped spread the feminist cause not only in the United States but also in other parts of the world. For many, Gloria has been the poster child of second-wave feminism. However, this fame has often come at a price and she has had to navigate various controversies throughout her life.

53. The Burden of Being a "Pretty" Woman and Feminist

Even before Gloria was known as a feminist, she was treated as a "pretty girl" by the people around her, especially when she was starting out as a journalist. Once, when she was sent to cover Bobby Kennedy's campaign along with novelist Saul Bellow and journalist Gay Talese, Talese told Bellow that Gloria was the latest in the list of pretty girls who come to New York each year and pretend to be a writer (Steinem, 2015). Even after Gloria had garnered some acclaim as a writer and journalist, she had to deal with rejections from editors of reputed magazines. One such editor of a national magazine told Gloria that they weren't looking for a pretty girl but a writer.

For most of her life, Gloria had to deal with two kinds of behavior which seemed different on the surface but which really stemmed from the same place of objectification of women. On one hand, people didn't take her or her many achievements seriously because she was conventionally good-looking. On the other hand, she was accused of benefiting from "pretty privilege" and using her looks to her advantage.

Even after she found some fame as a feminist, she was constantly called "beautiful" and her looks were a source of constant discussion and speculation. As Gloria matured as a woman and a feminist, she understood that the same people who equated all feminists to lesbians (because no one who wanted a man would also want autonomy) also expected all feminists to be "ugly." After all, if they were attractive enough to get a man, why would they fight for things like equality and liberation?

Over time, she gained confidence in her abilities and her purpose, and she also received support from other women when she traveled. During one such instance, where a reporter was trying to focus on her looks more than her message, an older woman in the audience comforted her by saying that someone needs to play the game and win so that they can say "The game ain't worth shit" (Steinem, 2015).

54. Controversy Surrounding Gloria's Earlier Views on Trans People and Their Rights

In August 1977, when U.S. tennis player Renée Richards participated in the U.S. Open as a woman, she made history as the first and only transgender player to participate in the men's and women's tournaments. Her road to being able to participate in the tournament was beset with numerous difficulties and even when she was able to embrace her identity and play as a woman, she had to face a lot of backlash from the media and anti-trans personalities.

It was against this background that Gloria published an anti-trans article called "If the Shoe Doesn't Fit, Change the Foot." In the article, she talked about transsexuals surgically mutilating their bodies "in order to set their real human personalities free" (James, 2024). She seemed to blame them for giving too much power to gender roles in society and also echoed some of the controversial statements made by Janice Raymond, who is a trans-exclusionary radical feminist.

However, in 2013, she apologized for the previous article and made amends through another piece published in the Advocate (James, 2024). She clarified that the words she had used in that article reflected a different time and were the result of some of the fears of queer people around her at the time. At the same time, she unequivocally stated that she supported transgender rights and believed that people who have transitioned are "living out real, authentic lives." She also affirmed that she believed that only trans people had the right to make choices regarding their bodies and their healthcare. In fact, she went on to state that trans people had many of the same challenges that cis women did, though they faced more discrimination and cruelty in general. She ended the beautiful essay by reaffirming her belief that "Humans are not ranked; we are linked."

In 2021, she went a step further by signing an open letter in solidarity with trans girls and women, along with many other feminist leaders. Not only did she show her support for trans women and girls, but she also denounced the people who used feminism to target trans people.

55. The Racism Versus Sexism Controversy in 2008

During the 2008 elections, history was made as the US had, for the first time ever, the possibility of electing either its first Black or the first female president. Gloria—along with many other feminists—was understandably excited at the idea of seeing a woman rule the country for the first time. She was actively involved in campaigning for Hillary Clinton, and she had witnessed the unique challenges she faced simply because she was a woman: the questions posed to her by the media, the assumptions made by both men and women of the general public, and even the extreme and irrational hate she was sometimes subjected to by women who should have otherwise empathized with her.

Perhaps fueled by these observations, she wrote a piece for the *New York Times* called "A Short History of Change." However, it was published as "Women Are Never Front-Runners" (Steinem, 2008). The main objective of the article was to make readers wonder why the question of gender-based discrimination in elections was not taken as seriously as the race-based one. The essay is well-argued on the whole and received initial praise from readers but after a while, many readers and journalists began to criticize Gloria for apparently saying that gender was more important than race in terms of the discrimination faced by the people of the country.

While this is not at all what Gloria meant, she did admit that using the phrase "Gender is probably the most restrictive force in American life" could have signaled otherwise to the readers. While she was shaken and hurt by the experience, she also acknowledged that even the most well-meaning words can have a different impact on others and that it's probably not a good idea to write when one is "angry and under deadline" (Steinem, 2015).

56. Implications of Lack of Support Toward Young Women

During the 2016 election campaign, when Gloria was supporting Hillary against Bernie Sanders at a New Hampshire rally, she and diplomat Madeleine Albright appeared to chastise young women who might have been supporting Bernie. While Albright said that "there is a special place in hell for women who don't help each other" (Rappeport, 2016), Gloria seemed to imply that any young woman who was supporting Bernie was doing so because the "boys are with Bernie."

This did not go down well with many young women. They felt that shaming them for their choices and essentially calling them stupid was not going to help Gloria and others win their vote. However, Gloria promptly apologized for her statements and reaffirmed her belief that no matter who they chose, more young women were activists and feminists than ever before.

57. Alleged Connection to the Central Intelligence Agency

In 1975, John D. Lofton—a conservative political commentator and journalist—accused Gloria of having been a CIA operative in the 1950s and '60s. The truth, as it turned out, is a little more nuanced than that. During the time period mentioned, Gloria was working with an organization called the Independent Research Service, which is known to be a front for the CIA. However, she was a part of the National Student Association, and her main role was to organize youth groups to attend two World Youth Festivals in Vienna and Helsinki respectively.

While she faced flak due to her association with the CIA—albeit indirectly—she defended her connection by saying that the agency was very different from its public image and that she found it honorable, nonviolent, and liberal.

58. Conflicts With Other Feminists Over the Years

Even though Gloria has made friends all over the world because of her feminist beliefs and work, she has also had her fair share of conflicts with other feminists. One of the most common criticisms she has faced over the years is that she has used the movement to promote herself and her glamorous image. These statements are hurtful no matter who says it but to hear fellow feminists hurl these accusations can be extremely disheartening. Also, ever since Gloria published a piece regarding her stint as an undercover Playboy bunny, she has come up against accusations from fellow feminists regarding her seriousness as a feminist.

Certain feminists, like the writer Vivian Gornick, have labeled themselves as radical feminists and called her an "uptown feminist" (Marchese, 2020). While Gloria recognizes this as an attempt to label her as White and elitist, she doesn't see any real worth to their claims.

When Gloria became the spokesperson for the Democratic convention at NWPC in 1972, she had to contend with Betty Friedan's anger and contempt. However, the problems with Betty ran much deeper. For instance, Bella Azbug once told her that the goal of the movement was not to replace the "White, male, middle-class elite" with the "White, female, middle-class elite" (Steinem, 2015). This enraged Betty, who accused them of being anti-elites. Not only that, but Betty was angry that the movement promoted lesbianism and even hatred of men, and that it was overly focused on mothers who were on welfare, as well as on others in the margins. She even blamed Gloria for using *Ms.* magazine to benefit from the movement.

While Bella was able to retort and eventually put Betty in her place, Gloria realized that she had a habit of avoiding conflict as much as possible. She was also wary of letting the media use their conflict to promote the tired trope that "women couldn't get along with each other" (Steinem, 2015).

Gloria has also had her differences with gender studies scholar and philosopher Judith Butler. She accepts that Judith's work can lead to enlightening conclusions, but she (Gloria) doesn't have much use for theory. Her path is one where she gets out of the world she knows and listens to the stories of other women. Therefore, she finds theory can often be excluding of others.

59. The Lands' End Controversy and Gloria's Brand

Over the years, Gloria has established herself as a fierce feminist icon who speaks her mind and knows what she stands for. This often works in her favor because she is approached by brands and organizations that want to clearly align themselves with her feminist beliefs. Once in a while, however, it also leads to controversy.

In 2016, a popular American retailer of girl's and women's clothing published an interview with Gloria Steinem in one of its catalogs. The interview was a part of the company's Legend Series, which focused on people who had made a difference in their respective fields as well as in the world. Gloria was one of the personalities featured in this series. However, when the interview was published, the retailer faced a lot of criticism from pro-life advocates for featuring someone who has always been pro-abortion. Many of them threatened to boycott the brand entirely. Perhaps more worryingly for them, there were certain private religious schools that threatened to stop ordering their school uniforms from the brand.

As a result, the brand pulled this piece from the magazine and apologized to their customers. They said that they didn't intend to raise a "divisive political or religious issue" (Brait, 2016) through this piece. After this decision, however, they had to face flak from many pro-choice activists as well as from feminist women. They were called out for not supporting women's right to equality and for taking what was seen as a cowardly stance.

60. Her Struggles With Cancer

Even though Gloria has lived a long and considerably active life, she has also had her fair share of health challenges. In 1987, she was diagnosed with breast cancer for the first time. She was understandably scared, more so because, at the time, she hadn't heard about older women who had survived breast cancer and lived a long, healthy life afterward. She was 52 when the cancer was discovered and even as she was undergoing treatment for it, she was also trying to make peace with the possibility of death. At the time, she thought that she was going to die and she convinced herself that she had had a wonderful life.

However, she survived and lived to see many more years before her cancer came back in 2013. This time, she had serious doubts that she was going to die, maybe because she had survived the ordeal once and that had given her confidence to deal with it again. Despite these challenges, Gloria has been able to live fully and purposefully even as she grows older.

61. Gloria's Views on Today's Cancel Culture

In July 2020, Gloria—along with other famous writers and thinkers like Margaret Atwood and Salman Rushdie—signed "A Letter of Justice and Open Debate," which was published by *Harper's Magazine*. She believes that, especially due to the prevalence of internet discourse, there is undue focus on what people say rather than on what they do.

According to her, if someone doesn't say what others believe to be right, they are met with hostility instead of an invitation to truly understand what they mean. While she understands being against someone's actions or statements, she also believes that by shunning the person who said or did something untoward, we are essentially shutting down the conversation and alienating those we want to either understand or change. What is important is that crucial conversations must go on for as long as possible.

62. What Does Gloria Think of the Criticisms She Has Faced Over the Years?

True to her form, Gloria has always been humble in the face of criticism and she has also welcomed it as a way for her to grow and evolve. In some cases, she makes peace with the fact that some people will criticize anyone who tries to create change. In such cases, she can move on after admitting that this is part of the deal for a public figure, especially a feminist one. In other instances, she acknowledges that criticism can be a form of projection. In other words, someone who has seen patriarchy or racism as a default all their lives might feel offended and angry when things begin to change around them. In those scenarios, criticism can mean that she's doing something right.

However, Gloria also acknowledges that she can make mistakes like everyone else. When she is criticized for the right reasons, it helps her course correct and make changes where necessary. As someone who has often been criticized for being a White feminist, Gloria also ensures that she shows up to events and promotes causes with partners who are women of color.

Chapter 8:

Friendships and Relationships—

How Has Her Personal Life

Affected Her Work and Public

Persona?

As a traveling feminist organizer and writer, Gloria has had the opportunity to make friends wherever she goes. Through her work at *Ms.* magazine, as well as through various organizations that she has co-founded and supported over the years, she has fostered relationships that have lasted an entire lifetime. How have these friendships and relationships affected her work and life as a feminist, and vice versa?

63. Her Friendship With Dorothy Pitman Hughes

Throughout her life, Gloria has spoken about the importance of having a chosen family. One of the most important members of her chosen family was Dorothy Pitman Hughes. Dorothy was a vital part of the women's liberation movement but she was so much more than that. She was a fantastic public speaker, a small business owner, a singer, and an activist who believed in the shared goals of race, class, and gender struggles. She was also a civil rights pioneer and someone who helped promote early childhood education and shelters for survivors of domestic violence.

Gloria met Dorothy when she was still working at the *New York Times* and had just published her article "After Black Power, Women's Liberation" in 1969. At the time, Dorothy was working to set up a multiracial and nonsexist child care center in New York to support working parents. As it turned out, Gloria was living near the center. She showed up one day to write an article on it and that is where the two met for the first time. At the time, she witnessed Dorothy use her kindness and warmth to encourage a small boy to believe in himself.

On another occasion, they met a man from a traditional Italian–American family who didn't believe in the divisions of race and class but had difficulty looking beyond gender divisions—especially when it came to letting his wife work after they were married. When they engaged in conversation with him, they were surprised to see that they could, in fact, change his point of view. Slowly, they began to work as a team and even considered talking to larger groups of people, especially women, about feminism in the child care center and later, in churches, school basements, suburban theaters, welfare centers, and even high school gyms.

Eventually, they were approached by two women from a lecture bureau to lead discussions for women who were interested in the liberation movement. Since Gloria was terrified of public speaking at the time, she was grateful to have Dorothy by her side. Together, they spoke of their parallel yet distinct experiences, and Dorothy would take over whenever Gloria froze or flagged her in for help. Also, because Gloria was White and Dorothy was Black, they were able to attract more diverse audiences than if either of them had been speaking individually.

Later, when Dorothy started her business (as well as a movement against gentrification) through a stationery shop in Harlem and became a mother, she traveled less frequently than before. When she did travel, the baby would go with her and they would each take turns looking after the baby as the other one spoke. As Dorothy traveled less and later moved to Florida, they weren't able to work or speak together as they had before, but they remained close friends until she passed away in 2022.

64. A Historical Portrait of Intersectional Feminism and Friendship

In 1971, Dan Wynn—a brilliant photographer and film director—took an iconic photo of Gloria and Dorothy together, their fists raised in the air. At the time, this photo was featured in *Esquire* and slowly became an important aspect of the intersectionality of the women's liberation movement. As a nod to its importance, it was later hung in the Smithsonian National Museum of African American History and Culture in Washington, D.C. In 2014, to commemorate Gloria's 80th birthday, Dorothy commissioned a reenactment of the original photograph in black-and-white by photographer Dan Bagan.

65. Florynce Kennedy—a Friend, Mentor, and Formidable Speaking Partner to Gloria

Florynce "Flo" Kennedy was another brilliant friend and partner who helped make the feminist movement intersectional in the 70s and 80s. She was the first Black woman to graduate from Columbia Law School in 1952, after which she practiced law by opening her own firm. She was 18 years older than Gloria and spent most of her adult life campaigning against racism in advertising, advocating for civil rights, and challenging New York state's abortion law. She also worked closely with Shirley Chisholm—another feminist—and nominated her as the president of the Feminist Party founded by her.

When Dorothy stepped back from her speaking engagements with Gloria, Flo stepped in and became her new speaking partner. For Gloria, traveling with Flo was an education in itself. Under her guidance, Gloria began to see not only how important it was for the feminist movement to be intersectional but also how the media discriminated against both of them in slightly different ways. For instance, when they would talk to reporters, they realized that Gloria would be asked questions related to gender while Flo would be asked questions about race. It was as if they could only understand one thing and not the other. She also witnessed the discrimination that Flo sometimes faced on airplanes and supported her by standing up to the often subtle but always hurtful behavior handed out to Flo.

Flo was the one who encouraged Gloria to not worry too much about "proving" the existence of discrimination to others but rather to work toward eliminating it. Flo also helped her see that criticism every once in a while could keep her sensitive (in more colorful language than this). Even after Flo passed away in 2000, her lessons in generosity, humor, and confidence have continued to inform Gloria's life in multiple ways.

66. Dolores Huerta and Gloria Steinem— Unlikely Allies at the Intersection of Gender, Class, and Labor

Before Dolores Huerta's and Gloria Steinem's paths crossed, they were both engaged in seemingly disparate movements. While Gloria was just beginning her journey as a feminist writer, Dolores was protesting alongside labor leader and activist César Chavez to start the National Farm Workers Association. When she first started out, her focus was on the mostly Mexican farm workers in California, and she didn't see feminism as something she needed to embrace to achieve her goals. More importantly, she felt that mainstream feminism was only concerned with white and upper-middle-class women and therefore, she didn't identify with the movement.

In 1965, she traveled to New York City to lead the National Boycott of California Table Grapes. While she wanted more women to join these protests, she didn't particularly expect feminists to join her cause. All that changed when Gloria became a vocal champion of the boycott and when she got Huntington Hartford—the heir of A&P supermarkets—to join the protest in support of farm workers. It was during this protest that Dolores, Dorothy, and Gloria protested together, and Dolores chanted her now-famous slogan *"Sí se puede,"* which means "Yes, we can" (Gutterman, 2020).

When the protests began to show results, she realized that the same women who had protested alongside her were not given a chance to lead the unions and organizations that were formed after the changes were implemented. She realized that feminism would help her fight for women's rights within the labor movement as well, giving them access to better wages and an equal say in unions. She famously called herself a "born again feminist" (Truffaut-Wong, 2017) and mentored young female activists all over the United States.

67. Wilma Mankiller and Gloria at the Intersection of Gender Equality and Indigenous Rights

Wilma Pearl Mankiller was a Native American activist, social worker, and feminist who was elected as the first woman to serve as the Principal Chief of the Cherokee Nation. Wilma grew up in Oklahoma but was forced to relocate to San Francisco with her family when she was 10. As she became interested in both civil rights and women's liberation movements in the 1960s, she also became aware of the discrimination she faced as an Indigenous person. When she separated from her first husband in 1977, she took her two teenage daughters and went back to the land she felt so deeply connected to and started working to improve the conditions of the people living there.

After a decade of working for the people around her—and achieving considerable acclaim for her work—she decided to stand for elections, something that was extremely rare for women of the Cherokee Nation.

Two years earlier, in 1985, she had met Gloria when the latter requested she join the board of the Ms. Foundation. Gloria had been inspired by Wilma's ability to help people achieve independence in their lives and knew that the foundation would benefit from her leadership.

During the elections, Gloria once again took on the role of a campaigner, but she gave all the credit for the win to Wilma and her years of tireless work. In 1991, Wilma became Principal Chief once again with an overwhelming majority, and in 2000, she was awarded the Presidential Medal of Freedom. According to Gloria, Wilma had all the makings of a great president herself if history had favored her.

Wilma also benefited from her association with *Ms.*, as it made it easier for her to come to terms with her own experience of past sexual assault. Gloria also talks about the humor and strength with which she faced all the challenges that came her way—be it regarding her health or otherwise. When she was politely questioned by people about her name, she would explain that it was a name given to the one who protects the group. When they asked in a rude or derisive manner, she would retort by saying, "I earned it" (Steinem, 2010). When she passed away in 2010, Gloria wrote a touching tribute for her in *TIME*, calling her "a symbol of hope for original cultures and movements around the world.

68. Gloria's Friendship With Alice Walker

Gloria has found a lifelong friend and colleague in writer and activist Alice Walker. In February 2014, a PBS documentary called *Alice Walker: Beauty in Truth* was released to honor her life and work. On this occasion, and on several others, Gloria has taken the opportunity to tell the world about her relationship with Alice and the inspiration she receives as her friend. In 1975, Alice became the editor of *Ms.* magazine. Despite being a solitary person and not attending a lot of editorial meetings, she created an indelible impact on the magazine.

Most importantly, she helped bring much-deserved attention to African writers like Zola Neale Hurston and Bessie Head. Alice and Gloria have also visited and spent time in the Cherokee Nation with Wilma and Deborah Mathews—a friend of Alice's who had a Cherokee great-grandmother.

According to Gloria, Alice's writing and activism are one and the same, which makes her true in every sense of the word. She believes that there is no demarcation between Alice's public and private selves and thinks of her as a spiritual mother, teacher, and dance partner. Alice has taught Gloria to be authentic in everything she does, to be aware of the means used to achieve her ends, to act as if every single thing matters, and to be a truth-teller in every sense of the word.

69. The Bond Between Gloria and Ruth Bader Ginsburg

Gloria knew Ruth long before she became the associate justice of the U.S. Supreme Court in 1993. Both were activists and feminists before they met, and Ruth was instrumental in creating the Women's Rights Project at the American Civil Liberties Union (ACLU). This is where Gloria first met her. Even as a young lawyer, Ruth played an important role in two feminist causes. One of them was the overturning of *Goesaert v. Cleary,* a Supreme Court case that prohibited women from bartending in any establishment in a city with a population of 50,000 or more. They could only do so if their husband or father owned the establishment.

When a journalism student named Joan Kennedy decided to drink at a bar with her mother and some friends in Syracuse, New York, and was turned away, she decided to challenge the law and asked the feminist group NOW to help. It took a bit of convincing for all the members to understand why this issue was an important one, but once they did, they started protesting outside and even inside certain bars. Among the people protesting was Gloria Steinem. Ruth, for her part, helped overturn *Goesaert v. Cleary* by using the help of another discrimination case. This way, both Ruth and Gloria contributed toward making bars accessible to women.

Ruth was always a vocal supporter of reproductive rights, but what most people forget is that she was not only against forced birth but also forced sterilization, especially of Black women. Gloria and Brenda—who was also her co-director at the Women's Rights Project—were asked to build a case by interviewing Fannie Lou Hammer, a great civil rights activist who was forcefully sterilized in a hospital that she had visited for a different purpose. Fannie's testimony helped build a strong case for Ruth, thus making it possible for her to save two teenage Black girls from being sterilized in return for state aid.

Over the years, Gloria was witness to Ruth's humor and compassion and Ruth's daughter even volunteered at *Ms.* Even though they were busy as their respective careers took off (an understatement), they remained close friends till Ruth passed away in 2020. On the occasion of her death, Gloria wrote a touching tribute for her, in which she said that if we could truly ask ourselves "What would Ruth do?" when faced with a challenge, her acts could guide us on the right path. It's what she continues to do in her own life (Steinem, 2020).

70. Gloria's Earlier Views on Marriage

The first marriage that Gloria witnessed was her parents', and while she loved both a lot and they were good parents to her in their own ways, she could never understand how two fundamentally different people could ever have married in the first place. It was difficult for her to see how marriage benefited women and that shaped her views on marriage for a long time. Despite knowing that marriage didn't really work for women, she thought for a long time that she would have to get married, as she didn't know that another reality could exist for women. Also, her itinerant childhood made her crave a stable home, which, at the time included a husband and kids.

When she was still in college, she was engaged to someone who she realized was not the right person for her. As she progressed on her journey as a feminist writer and organizer, she began to see how unequal marriage could really be for most women. This prompted her to take what seemed to be an antimarriage stance. Some of her quotes around marriage include, "Legally speaking, it was designed for a person-and-a-half. You became a semi non-person when you got married" and "The surest way to be alone is to get married" (Associated Press, 2000). She also urged girls and young women to focus on their careers through quotes such as, "Some of us are becoming the men we wanted to marry" (Steinem, 2004).

71. Her Marriage to David Bale, the Media's Reaction to It, and Her Changing Views on Marriage

When the world's most famous feminist got married to South Africa-born entrepreneur David Bale—who also happens to be actor Christian Bale's father—in a small ceremony in rural Oklahoma in 2000, the world went into a frenzy. People were surprised, to say the least, and many conservative media outlets took the opportunity to subtly and not-so-subtly ridicule Gloria for what was seen as an abandonment of her earlier views on marriage. For many antifeminists, this was seen as a decision that somehow proved no one could live without marriage.

When asked about this, Gloria answered in a way that proved she predicted this kind of backlash. In response to speculations that she and David had only gotten married for visa purposes, she said that since she was a feminist, it was important for others to look for ulterior motives behind her decision to marry. When asked if she had changed her mind about marriage, she clarified that she had never been against marriage. Instead, when she embarked on her journey as a feminist, marriage looked very different from what it was then (Napikoski, 2019a). Her work as a feminist had contributed toward making marriage a better deal for many women, which is why it didn't feel like a bad idea to her then.

While she would have lost most of her civil rights if she had married in the 50s and 60s, she was able to retain her autonomy in her marriage, which was very important to her. Add to that, she was marrying someone she truly loved and respected—someone who was a feminist and activist in his own right. The marriage took place at Wilma's home and was presided over by an Oklahoma judge and Charlie Soap, who happened to be Wilma's husband. To keep its egalitarian spirit intact, the term "husband and wife" was substituted by "partners."

Even though she lost him to an illness just three years after she had married him when she was 66 years old, she regrets nothing about marrying him when she did and she has only fond memories of the man she loved and lived with as a true partner.

Chapter 9:

Gloria Steinem as a Media Figure—How Her Work Has Enriched the Intellectual and Political Landscape.

Gloria Steinem's work as a writer and media personality has left a mark not only on the feminist movement but also on various other aspects of society. She has lobbied for more female representation in the media and has used her platform to shine a light on stories that otherwise don't receive the attention they deserve.

72. Gloria's Work in the Field of Child Abuse

In 1993, Gloria had an idea for a documentary to highlight the effects of child abuse on both men and women. This led her to coproduce and narrate an Emmy award-winning TV documentary with HBO called *Multiple Personalities: The Search for Deadly Memories* (Voros, 1993). The idea behind this documentary was to chronicle the lives of three survivors of childhood physical and sexual abuse and to show how years of violent abuse have left them prone to dissociate into multiple personalities. The camera follows these survivors who either revisit their childhood abuse or adopt an alter ego who helps them cope with the trauma of abuse. While it's not recommended viewing for everybody, it does a commendable job of understanding people with multiple personality disorders as survivors of excruciatingly difficult childhoods.

73. A Story About Race, Abortion, and the Death Penalty

Also in 1993, Gloria also became executive producer on a Lifetime movie called *Better Off Dead*. The idea came about when Gloria realized that the same forces that oppose legal abortion are the ones that push for capital punishment. This was something she wanted to explore as she had not really seen such stories on screen. She also chose TV as her medium because she felt that feature films often avoid difficult subjects such as this one.

She also wanted to make a TV movie where women were neither used as token characters nor were they shown fighting with each other. Instead, she wanted to show women, especially those of different races, working together for a common cause. Most importantly, both Gloria and her partner on this project—Rosilyn Heller—wanted a Black director for the project. According to Gloria, it was very important that the project be helmed by a Black person as they would be aware of Black people's lives and experiences. The result was an intriguing project that tackled various sensitive topics with assurance.

74. Gloria's Travels in Search of Stories of Women Facing Violence

Combining her lifelong love for travel, her fearless search for stories, and her quest to uncover the links between gender and violence through an intersectional lens, Gloria went to different parts of the world and tried to understand the experiences of women in each of those countries. These experiences came together in a hard-hitting 2016 documentary called *Woman* that premiered on VICELAND (*Woman*, n.d.). However, these aren't simply stories of desperation and violence—they also show how women in dire circumstances are resisting the patterns of violence and trying to carve out a different future for themselves.

The eight-episode series covers the child brides of Zambia as well as the effect of extremist violence in Pakistan on its women. It highlights the prevalence of sexual assault in the U.S. military and the measures being taken to combat the issue. Similarly, it shows how rape is often used as a war tactic, and how the women of First Nations in Canada are being kidnapped and murdered at alarming rates. The much-lauded series was nominated for two Emmy awards.

75. Women's Media Center—Ensuring Women's Visibility in Media

Gloria's feminist work made it clear to her that the stories that needed to be told—of women and other marginalized groups—were not being given the platform they needed. Just as she had started *Ms.* in 1971 to ensure that women's stories were being told by the women themselves—and to lay the foundation for a feminist media organization—she decided to go a step further in 2005.

Women's Media Center (WMC) was started by Robin Morgan, Gloria Steinem, and actress Jane Fonda to give more women decision-making powers in media. This would ensure that the voices of girls and women were heard. One aspect of the organization is focused on various content channels like *WMC Women Under Siege*, WMC Features, and WMC Speech Project. The aim is to create and promote stories that are either ignored or misrepresented in mainstream media.

Another aspect is concerned with producing and distributing various research publications that cast a light on various women-centric topics that are not discussed or analyzed enough. For instance, one publication focuses on how U.S. media covers campus rape and assault, while another discusses the gender gap in the coverage of reproductive issues in the US. The third aspect of WMC deals with the training and development of women in media—helping them hone their skills, land roles, and connect to the right people in various organizations.

76. The Connection Between the Media and the Movement

In 2003, Gloria Steinem contributed a piece called *The Media and the Movement: A User's Guide* as part of an anthology called *Sisterhood Is Forever: The Women's Anthology for a New Millennium* (Morgan, 2003). In this piece, she talked about the importance of using both alternative and mainstream media to our advantage. She pointed out how the control and manipulation of media are often one of the first things done by dictators. Therefore, if we—that is, women and other marginalized communities—want our stories to be told in the right way, we need to learn to monitor and replace harmful media and also to create new forms of representing reality.

In this compelling essay, she brought attention to the numerous ways in which the movement has changed the media. Through various examples, she showed how the media often reflects the state of society, as it did before the women's liberation movement. She also showed how powerful forces use the media to distort reality and undermine the feminist movement. At the end of her piece, she urged everyone to derive strength from the success of previous movements and to use new media to shape the future of the current movement.

Chapter 10:

Awards and Honors—Recognition for Decades of Path-Breaking Work

It's next to impossible to measure the true impact of Gloria's work through the decades. Even though she has been awarded and honored by numerous prestigious organizations and even by governments, her true reward has been in bearing witness to the progress of the women's movement.

77. Awards for Writing and Journalism

Gloria's writing and journalism have helped create awareness around many feminist issues, and they have also inspired a whole generation of writers and journalists to be intrepid in their search for the truth. For her writing and journalism, she has received numerous awards—such as the Society of Writers Award from the United Nations, the Front Page and Clarion Awards, the Penney-Missouri Journalism Award, the University of Missouri School of Journalism Award for Distinguished Service in Journalism, the National Magazine Award, the Lifetime Achievement in Journalism Award from the Society of Professional Journalists, and an Emmy Citation for excellence in television writing.

When asked to give advice to the next generation of writers and journalists, Gloria lists numerous reasons why journalism is a profession like no other. She starts with things like journalism is a "portable" profession, but then talks about how it's a profession where we get paid to learn. She urges the next generation to think carefully about their power to make the "invisible visible"—by talking about topics that are otherwise not discussed or even discussed wrongly (Silurians Press Club, 2016). Eventually, it all comes down to how journalists and writers choose to wield the power they possess.

78. Recipient of the Presidential Medal of Freedom in 2013

Years earlier, Gloria had witnessed her late friend Wilma receive the Presidential Medal of Freedom for her work as an Indigenous feminist organizer and activist. In 2013, Gloria was bestowed this honor—the highest in the United States—by President Barack Obama. Before placing the medal around her neck, Obama talked about her many achievements in the field of women's liberation. She also received the award for her role in co-founding *Ms.* in 1971 and for her exceptional activism through initiatives like Take Our Daughters to Work Day. President Obama also noted that Gloria's work was instrumental in giving women across America and the world "the respect and opportunities that they deserve (*Remarks by the President at Presidential Medal of Freedom Ceremony*, 2013)."

After the honor, Gloria gave a speech at the Press Club, where she was the first woman to give a speech in 1971 after the club began accepting female members. Humble and gracious as always, Gloria said that it would be insane if she didn't understand the medal belonged to the entire women's liberation movement (Kort, 2013).

79. Recipient of the Eleanor Roosevelt Val-Kill Medal in 2014

When Gloria was a young girl, her mother's stories usually involved her struggles during the Great Depression and her gratitude toward the Roosevelts for bringing the country out of that dark period. She grew up learning about the ways in which Franklin and Eleanor empathized with the lives of those who existed at the bottom of society even though they themselves belonged to the top. Her mother told her about how she got through the Great Depression with bravery by listening to President Roosevelt's speeches on her radio.

Needless to say, the Roosevelts had been a source of inspiration to Gloria even before she embarked on her journey as a feminist. Therefore, it was an extremely special moment for Gloria when she was awarded the Eleanor Roosevelt Val-Kill Medal in 2014 for being an "extraordinary social justice activist" (Omega Institute, 2013). In her acceptance speech, Gloria talked about her dedication to upholding Eleanor's legacy of promoting human rights and social justice. She even joked that she planned to live a very long life so she could continue the work she had been doing all her life.

80. Recipient of Spain's Prestigious Award in 2021

In 2021, Gloria was awarded Spain's prestigious Princess of Asturias Award for Humanities and Communication. The jury decided to award Gloria because of her activism within the women's liberation movement—for her commitment to feminism as well as her focus on intersectionality and equality within her activism.

In her acceptance speech (Steinem, 2021), Gloria talked about how the COVID-19 pandemic had made national and international boundaries seem a bit useless and how it had united people all over the world in anxiety. She also talked about the ways in which staying at home had brought fathers closer to their children and helped them appreciate the labor that goes into childcare. However, the same lockdown had also caused an increase in domestic violence in certain places and there was also an increase in racial attacks during that time. While she talked about the challenges and concerns regarding the pandemic, she also discussed the things that gave her hope.

She was grateful for receiving an award that had once been given to writers and revolutionaries like Doris Lessing and Nelson Mandela. She was especially pleased about receiving the first prize of her life given in another woman's honor. She ended the speech by talking about laughter as proof of freedom. She pointed out how dictators and fascists over the years have been most scared of being laughed at because they know that laughter cannot be forced. Therefore, she encouraged everyone in the audience to preserve their freedom to laugh.

81. International Advocate for Peace Award in 2023

In March 2023, Gloria was awarded the International Advocate for Peace Award by the Cardozo Journal of Conflict Resolution at Cardozo Law School. By accepting this award, she joined a long list of distinguished awardees like President Jimmy Carter, Reverend Desmond Tutu, and Paul McCartney. She was given the award for furthering the cause of peace throughout her work as a feminist writer and organizer.

She talked about how, as a woman, she is used to thinking of most conflicts "from a family perspective," meaning she wants to listen to each party and make everyone feel heard in a dispute. At the same time, she said that repressive systems often demand revolutions, and that true change comes from "changing the hearts and minds of individuals" (*Feminist leader Gloria Steinem*, 2023).

She ended her conversation by saying that even during dark times, she derived hope by being in a room full of young people like those who were present in the audience, who were energetic and hopeful about creating change in the future. She was also thanked by the dean of the school, who said that Gloria served as an inspiration to her growing up and helped her imagine a different future for herself.

82. Gloria: In Her Own Words—Inspiring the Next Generation of Feminists

Even though Gloria has been a tireless feminist and activist for most of her life, some of her admirers believe that the younger generation needs to know her on a deeper level. While Gloria has always been very honest about how she is only part of the women's liberation movement and has tried to avoid being cast as the singular force for the movement, it cannot be denied that she has contributed immensely toward making it a mainstream movement in the 70s and 80s.

Among her many admirers is Sheila Nevins, who in 2015, was the president of HBO's documentary film division. According to her, Gloria was the most important woman she had ever met apart from her mother. She wanted the next generation to know who Gloria really was, and thus, she decided to release a documentary about her life made by putting together hours and hours of archival footage.

When Gloria saw the final result, she was surprised at how much of her own life she had forgotten and also at how young and vulnerable she seemed in some of the footage. While she couldn't say then what impact the film would have on its viewers, she was grateful that the producers had taken an interest in her life and asked her questions that made her feel heard.

While there were many reasons for Sheila to admire Gloria, the main reason was the encounter she had had with her almost 20 years prior to working with her on the documentary. When she had met her in Los Angeles and expressed her admiration for her work, Gloria had turned to her and asked her about herself. She had taken a genuine interest in her life and had taught her a lesson in how to treat others. Just like many others, Gloria had left an indelible impact on Sheila's life simply by being herself.

83. How Has Gloria Impacted the Lives of Other Feminists?

While there are many feminists who owe their activism to Gloria, there are a few who have written extensively about the lessons they've learned by watching her or sharing space with her. One of these feminists is Shelby Knox, who became famous as the subject of an award-winning 2005 documentary called *The Education of Shelby Knox*, which threw light on her teenage activism to promote queer rights and sex education in her conservative and religious community.

Throughout her life, she has been an organizer and has also spent some time with Gloria at her house when she first moved to New York. Knowing Gloria so closely has helped her learn numerous lessons over the years. She has learned from Gloria that sharing one's ideas is a gift, and getting credit for them is important but not as important as ensuring that those ideas make a movement better. Similarly, Gloria has urged Shelby to distance herself from theory and think in terms of the stories that affect her because that is where true connection happens. Additionally, Gloria has taught Shelby to trust herself at all times. Feminists like Shelby have found that even a few moments spent in Gloria's presence can become an education in themselves.

Chapter 11:

Gloria's Legacy, Her Advice to Women and Men, and Her Hopes for the Future

If you look at a feminist and an organizer who has been working for more than six decades, it's easy to wonder if they are still relevant in today's times. You might also believe that they are ready to finally slow down, but you would be wrong. As Gloria celebrates yet another milestone birthday, her lessons remain as relevant as ever, as does she. At the same time, she harbors hope for the future generation of writers, activists, and feminists.

84. Various Books Written by Her and Her Motivations Behind Them

It's impossible to talk about Gloria's legacy and not mention the amazing books she has written for all of us to better understand the movement as well as to be inspired to start our own. Gloria has famously said, "Writing is the only thing that, when I do it, I don't feel like doing something else" (Mullen-Brown, 2022). Apart from books like *My Life on the Road* and *As if Women Matter*, Gloria has published a few other bestsellers that continue to remain relevant today. One of them is the 1992 book *Revolution From Within,* in which Gloria wrote about the reasons why women have often been sidelined in history and how they can build their self-esteem to become the change they wish to see in their lives. Such was the impact of the book that Gloria still receives letters from people who have battled low self-esteem and emerged victorious after reading it.

In 1986, Gloria published a book called *Marilyn: Norma Jean*, in which she moved beyond the stereotypes that Marilyn Monroe was often subjected to. In many ways, she gave it a much-needed feminist and humane treatment and tried to undo the damage caused by prejudiced and hurtful narratives like the one by writer Norman Mailer. She helped readers see the real Norma Jean and tried to establish her as a complex and intelligent character in their minds.

In 1983, she published *Outrageous Acts and Everyday Rebellions,* her first book of essays. While it remains relevant today, Gloria wishes it didn't because it contained essays on topics such as the wage gap between men and women, female genital mutilation, and sexual harassment. The sad truth is that despite the progress women have made today, a lot more still needs to be done.

85. Her Views on the Progress Made in the Last 50 Years

One major sign of progress in the last 50 years has been that a greater proportion of women are now choosing to exercise their right to vote. She also believes that women have made progress in terms of their domestic rights by asking for more contribution and support from their male partners in chores and childrearing. At the same time, she feels like we are still fighting for these rights because enough progress hasn't been made in these aspects.

She has also been appalled at the curtailing of reproductive rights in the United States, almost 50 years after *Roe v. Wade* came into being. As someone who has always seen reproductive freedom as a fundamental right, Gloria is rightfully concerned about what it means for the future of feminism.

As an intersectional feminist, she has always been mindful of the struggles that women face in other parts of the world. She can look at those struggles and see similarities between them and other feminist struggles in the US or the world. In other words, Gloria believes that the work of feminism is far from over.

86. Her Faith in Young Women and Feminists of Today

Gloria is full of hope for the young women of today. She believes that young women are more confident in saying what they feel and are less likely to tolerate bad behavior from anyone. In general, she also feels that women today are more supportive of each other. However, she warns against getting complacent or allowing others to convince us that the feminist revolution is unnecessary or even over. In fact, she believes that we have at least another 50 years to go before the changes made in the last 50 years become permanent.

87. Embracing Men as Feminists

Gloria truly believes that the patriarchy causes a lot of damage to men as well. In fact, men often learn harmful rules regarding masculinity that prevent them from embracing their own tenderness. Therefore, feminism benefits both men and women by creating a world where our gender doesn't dictate what we can and cannot do. However, she also believes that it's not women's responsibility to urge men to become feminists. They should be ready for the fact that many men will reject feminism simply because it doesn't allow them to dominate women anymore.

According to Gloria, it can be helpful for both men and women to understand that patriarchy is not the default. In fact, the concept of gender—and gender roles—is relatively new. Many ancient cultures—

especially Indigenous ones—didn't have a concept of gender, or at least of gender inequality. Therefore, we might need to go way back to go forward.

88. Her Advice for Activists Who Want to Create Change

Gloria has always believed that true change cannot happen from the top down; instead, it can only happen from the bottom up. This is why she believes that change—at least for women—often begins at home. If women can assert themselves at home and in their personal relationships, then they can establish true democracy at home.

For those activists who want to do good in the world but are wondering where to start, Gloria has two important pieces of advice: One is that there's no point sitting around wondering what to do. Instead, one needs to start doing whatever they can in the moment. Another is to find people who share their values, otherwise they would feel isolated and hopeless in the face of injustice and setbacks. (Schnall, n.d.)

89. Feel-Good Advice From a Hopeaholic

Gloria understands, more than most, how intimidating it can be to fight for women's rights in today's landscape. Since there's so much that needs to be done, it is understandable that we feel bogged down by all the work. However, Gloria has some advice for all of us (Lunn, 2016). One, she wants us to celebrate our bodies each day. Two, she wants us to let go of regrets because regrets can sometimes lead to blessings and celebrations. And three, she wants us to dance as wildly and freely as possible. It helps that Gloria promises that the path to true gender equality will be fun and that she will be right there along with us.

90. Gloria's Views on Aging and Her Dreams for "Old Age"

While her views on aging are personal and unique to her, anyone, but especially women, can learn from them. When she turned 81, Gloria said that she wasn't unhappy about aging because she now felt "free from the demands of gender" (Gross, 2020). She compared life after 60 to life at 9 or 10 as a young girl, when she didn't think about her gender before deciding on activities or dreams. She felt the same way as she grew older and also felt like she could do whatever she wanted.

She also said that when she grows really old—she hopes to live past 100—she would love to have a little diner of her own. This is a dream she had when she was still a young girl traveling with her parents to sell antiques. According to her, diners are the "most democratic" and "truly populist" places. She also hopes that her diner will have a back room where people can participate in "revolutionary meetings" every now and then (Steinem, 1998).

Conclusion

One of the challenges of writing about someone as famous and as well-regarded as Gloria Steinem is feeling like there is, at once, not enough and too much to say. What can be said of someone who has been the subject of various profiles, documentaries, and even movies over the years? What can be revealed about someone who has lived most of their life in the public eye? More importantly, how can one decide what should and should not be highlighted when creating a portrait of a beloved feminist leader who has also had her share of challenges?

I knew why this book was important for me to write. I knew that I wanted to paint an intimate portrait of someone who has been as misunderstood as she has been supported, and who has been as much of an enigma as she has revealed herself to the public. I wanted to uncover the warm, kind, and self-effacing human being behind the phenomenal personality. I wanted the world to see what is possible through sheer determination and cautious optimism.

I had another reason for wanting to uncover 90 tales about Gloria Steinem. This world can often make us jaded and it can be difficult for us to find evidence of goodness and kindness in other human beings. Since Gloria had spent a large part of her childhood and even young adulthood trying to deal with her difficult circumstances, I wanted to show others how she made her way in a world that was often hostile to her. I wanted to tell stories about the friends she made along the way, the acts of kindness she encountered, and the lifelong relationships she formed even as she embarked on a difficult and often isolating path.

As I researched and began to write down the stories in this book, it became clear to me that I was not only recreating the portrait of a feminist and organizer, but I was also opening myself up to possibilities. Each story gave me strength and renewed faith in what we can achieve together. These stories helped me see the world in a different way, which is possibly the most powerful thing that any story can do.

Through these stories, I have tried to make you see the real Gloria Steinem, and I hope that you do. What I also hope is that you are able to find the courage and conviction you need to live a life that is authentic and full of joy. After all, Gloria's life has been all about finding joy and meaning in the little and not-so-little things, even as she has braved various challenges and difficulties while paving a path for women not only in the United States but all over the world.

Let's go over some of the things we've learned through these 90 remarkable tales:

- In the first chapter, we got to know Gloria as a child and young adult. We became familiar with her relationship with her parents, her early travels as a child, and the effect that these experiences had on her.

- In the second chapter, we followed Gloria as she tried to establish herself as a journalist and find her own voice. We learned about some milestones of her early journalism career and how they set the stage for her feminist organization work.

- In the third chapter, we learned about the motivations behind co-founding *Ms.* magazine, the challenges she faced along the way, and the impact of the magazine in the last 50 years.

- In the fourth chapter, we were introduced to Gloria the feminist organizer and campaign manager. We discussed the different experiences that shaped her political consciousness, the different kinds of organizing she did, and the allies and friends she made along the way.

- The fifth chapter was all about following Gloria on her travels across the world and understanding how those travels helped her become the feminist and human being she is today.

- In the sixth chapter, we looked at the various intersectional causes that Gloria championed throughout her life—the issues she tackled and the lessons she learned as she understood how various social and political struggles around the world were linked with each other.

- In the seventh chapter, we came to understand the various challenges and controversies faced by Gloria throughout her life as a feminist organizer and activist. We also learned about the ways in which she overcame these challenges and stayed true to her path.

- The eighth chapter was all about the various relationships and friendships that have enriched Gloria's life and how these have affected her work as a feminist and writer.

- In the ninth chapter, we examined how Gloria used the media to connect with the public and make them aware of the injustices that are faced by people around the world.

- In the tenth chapter, we looked at some of the main awards that Gloria has received throughout her life and what those awards mean for both her and the movement she has dedicated her life to.

- In the last chapter, we talked about Gloria's legacy, her views on the evolution of feminism, and her hope and advice for future generations.

I hope that *Gloria Steinem: 90 Remarkable Tales From 90 Extraordinary Years* has been as interesting for you to read as it was for me to research and write. The research I undertook on Gloria Steinem has definitely restored my faith in humanity and in the power of courage and compassion to overcome all the trials and tribulations that one may face on one's path. Lastly, I would be deeply grateful if you could take the time to leave me a review on Amazon, letting me know how you enjoyed the book and whether you were as inspired by Steinem's life as I was. I read every review and take any suggestions very seriously.

And, if you did enjoy this book, please look for my other biographies, including *Jimmy Carter: 99 Remarkable Tales From 99 Extraordinary Years* and *Jane Goodall: 90 Remarkable Tales From 90 Extraordinary Years*.

Author Bio

Anthony Dobbs is a best-selling biographer and historian with a passion for unraveling the lives of remarkable individuals. With work dedicated to chronicling the journeys of notable figures, Anthony has earned a reputation for digging deep into the rich tapestry of history and revealing the human stories that lie within.

In *Gloria Steinem: 90 Remarkable Tales From 90 Extraordinary Years*, Anthony brings his unparalleled storytelling prowess to the life and times of one of America's most influential figures in modern feminism. With meticulous research and an infallible eye for detail, he presents an intimate portrait of Gloria's unwavering commitment to social justice, equality, and empowerment.

Through her words, actions, and unwavering dedication to amplifying the voices of marginalized communities, Gloria has inspired generations of women and men to challenge the status quo and strive for a more just and equitable world. Anthony paints a vivid and comprehensive picture of this extraordinary woman in 90 wonderfully told narratives, offering intimate insights into Gloria's remarkable journey, illuminating the challenges she faced, the triumphs she achieved, and the profound impact she has had.

Anthony skillfully weaves together the threads of Gloria Steinem's experiences, offering readers a glimpse into the wisdom, resilience, and unwavering commitment that has defined her inspiring journey. In this deeply moving and informative book, Anthony invites readers to embark on a captivating journey through history, celebrating the life and legacy of this extraordinary and influential figure.

If you enjoyed this book, please look for Anthony's other biographies, including *Jimmy Carter: 99 Remarkable Tales From 99 Extraordinary Years* and *Jane Goodall: 90 Remarkable Tales From 90 Extraordinary Years*.

References

About WMC. (n.d.). Women's Media Center. https://womensmediacenter.com/about

About FMF - Feminist Majority Foundation. (2020, July 4). Feminist Majority Foundation. https://feminist.org/about/

About Ms. (2023, November 1). Ms. Magazine. https://msmagazine.com/about/

Agents of Social Change Online Exhibit - Women's Action Alliance. (n.d.). Sophia Smith Collection. https://www.smith.edu/libraries/libs/ssc/agents/waa.html

Alter, E. (2020, September 22). *Ruth Bader Ginsburg remembered by friend Gloria Steinem: "I thought she was immortal."* Yahoo! Entertainment. https://www.yahoo.com/entertainment/ruth-bader-ginsburg-remembered-by-friend-gloria-steinem-i-thought-she-was-immortal-172158956.html

Amidi, F., & Thorn, R. (2023, December 2). Gloria Steinem: Feminist icon on "lethal" desire to control wombs. *BBC News.* https://www.bbc.com/news/world-67445694

Associated Press. (2000, September 5). *Gloria Steinem says "I do."* CBS News. https://www.cbsnews.com/news/gloria-steinem-says-i-do/#textFor20years2C20Steinem20said20theperson20when20you20got20married22

Baker, C. N. (2022, December 14). *The story of iconic feminist Dorothy Pitman Hughes: "With her fist Raised".* Ms. Magazine. https://msmagazine.com/2021/09/09/dorothy-pitman-hughes-feminist-gloria-steinem-who-founded-ms-magazine/

Bennetts, L. (2013, September 4). *The philosophy of Gloria Steinem, patron saint of American feminism.* Vanity Fair.

https://www.vanityfair.com/culture/1992/01/gloria-steinem-feminism-book

Bio. (n.d.). Women's Media Center. https://womensmediacenter.com/profile/gloria-steinem

Brait, E. (2016, February 26). *Lands' End takes down interview with Gloria Steinem after customer backlash.* The Guardian. https://www.theguardian.com/books/2016/feb/26/gloria-steinem-lands-end-interview-abortion-backlash

Braver, R. (2023, September 17). *Ms. after 50: Gloria Steinem and a feminist publishing revolution.* CBS News. https://www.cbsnews.com/news/ms-magazine-gloria-steinem/

Brockes, E. (2015, October 17). Gloria Steinem: "If men could get pregnant, abortion would be a sacrament." *The Guardian.* https://www.theguardian.com/books/2015/oct/17/gloria-steinem-activist-interview-memoir-my-life-on-the-road

Brozan, N. (1990, April 9). *Telling the Seder's story in the voice of a woman.* The New York Times. https://www.nytimes.com/1990/04/09/nyregion/telling-the-seder-s-story-in-the-voice-of-a-woman.html

Cavanagh, J., & Bennis, P. (2021, September 10). *9/11 and after: The need is still for justice, not vengeance.* National Priorities Project. https://www.nationalpriorities.org/pressroom/articles/2021/09/10/911-need-still-for-justice-not-vengeance/

Coalition of Labor Union Women (CLUW). Encyclopedia Britannica. Retrieved on March 20, 2024 from https://www.britannica.com/topic/Coalition-of-Labor-Union-Women

Costa-Roberts, D. (2015, May 24). *Gloria Steinem, peace activists cross Demilitarized Zone separating Koreas.* PBS NewsHour. https://www.pbs.org/newshour/world/gloria-steinem-among-activists-crossed-dmz-north-south-korea

Cunningham, C. (n.d.). *Gloria Steinem's childhood on the road.* Sutori. https://www.sutori.com/it/storia/gloria-steinem-s-childhood-on-the-road--be8eBmJVxaTdASiqhm7VgV6w

Dininny, S. (2003, January 27). *50 years after the Kinsey report.* CBS News. https://www.cbsnews.com/news/50-years-after-the-kinsey-report/

Dismore, D. M. (2020, December 17). *Today in feminist history: Our feminism includes lesbians (December 17, 1970).* Ms. Magazine. https://msmagazine.com/2020/12/17/today-in-feminist-history-our-feminism-includes-lesbians-december-17-1970/

Doherty, M. (2023, December 11). *10 Ways Ms., Sassy, and Jezebel changed your life!* The Yale Review. https://yalereview.org/article/maggie-doherty-more-than-magazines

Dreier, P. (2016, February 20). *Gloria Steinem renews an old debate about socialism and feminism.* Dissent Magazine. https://www.dissentmagazine.org/blog/gloria-steinem-hillary-clinton-socialism-feminism-history/

Emory University. (2009, May 8). *Tribute to Alice Walker: Gloria Steinem* [Video]. YouTube. https://www.youtube.com/watch?v=ge_FI-dRmjs

Enzler, F. (2024, February 4). *Wrong on all counts: One woman's reflections on her 1976 coming out Letter to Ms.* Ms. Magazine. https://msmagazine.com/2018/01/30/coming-letter-sent-ms-40-years-later/

Equal Rights Amendment (ERA) | Definition, history, text, pros and cons, & facts. Encyclopedia Britannica. Retrieved on March 20, 2024 from https://www.britannica.com/topic/Equal-Rights-Amendment

Equality Now. (2020, March 25). *Gloria Steinem: 10 quotes from the front-lines of the fight for equality.*

https://equalitynow.org/news_and_insights/gloria_steinem_q
uotes/

Espeland, P. (2020, February 20). *Gloria Steinem on the ERA, #MeToo and hope.* MinnPost. https://www.minnpost.com/artscape/2020/02/gloria-steinem-on-the-era-metoo-and-hope/

Esther M. Broner. (n.d.). Jewish Women's Archive. https://jwa.org/encyclopedia/article/broner-esther-m#pid-11132

Feminist leader Gloria Steinem accepts the International Advocate for Peace Award at Cardozo. (2023, March 30). Cardozo Law. https://cardozo.yu.edu/news/feminist-leader-gloria-steinem-accepts-international-advocate-peace-award-cardozo

Feminist seder, 1991. (n.d.). Jewish Women's Archive. https://jwa.org/media/spirituality-2-still-image

Fessler, L. (2022, July 20). *Gloria Steinem says Black women have always been more feminist than White women.* Quartz. https://qz.com/1150028/gloria-steinem-on-metoo-black-women-have-always-been-more-feminist-than-white-women

Foussianes, C. (2021, November 2). *The true story of Ms. Magazine, and what it meant for feminist publishing.* Town & Country. https://www.townandcountrymag.com/leisure/arts-and-culture/a32131889/gloria-steinem-ms-magazine-true-story/

Galanes, P. (2020, September 8). *Ruth Bader Ginsburg and Gloria Steinem on the unending fight for women's rights.* The New York Times. https://www.nytimes.com/2015/11/15/fashion/ruth-bader-ginsburg-and-gloria-steinem-on-the-unending-fight-for-womens-rights.html

Global Risk Insights. (2022, March 9). *The fight for equality: An interview with Gloria Steinem.* https://globalriskinsights.com/2022/02/the-fight-for-equality-an-interview-with-gloria-steinem/

Gloria Steinem. (n.d.a). The Decision Lab. https://thedecisionlab.com/thinkers/political-science/gloria-steinem

Gloria Steinem. (n.d.b). Archives of Women's Political Communication. https://awpc.cattcenter.iastate.edu/directory/gloria-steinem/

Gloria's Foundation. (n.d.). *A movement lived and written.* Google Arts & Culture. https://artsandculture.google.com/story/vQVxnaZnaQeGjQ

Gloria Steinem: Restoring women's rights in Afghanistan. (2001, December 27). CNN. https://edition.cnn.com/2001/COMMUNITY/12/27/steinem.cnna/index.html

Gloria Steinem and Dorothy Pitman Hughes, 1971. (2016, December 3). Dan Wynn Archive. http://www.danwynn.com/blog/2016/12/3/gloria-steinem-and-dorothy-pitman-hughes-1971

Gross, T. (2020, September 25). *Feminist Gloria Steinem on finding herself free of the "Demands of gender."* NPR. https://www.npr.org/2020/09/25/916870127/feminist-gloria-steinem-on-finding-herself-free-of-the-demands-of-gender

Gutterman, A. (2020, September 30). *Beyond Gloria Steinem: What to know about the women of color who were instrumental to the Women's Liberation Movement.* TIME. https://time.com/5894877/glorias-movie-activists/

History and vision. (n.d.). We are linked not ranked. https://wearelinkednotranked.com/pages/history-and-vision

Hogan, L. S. (1999). *Gloria Steinem, "living the revolution" (31 MAY 1970)* (Vols. 66–78) [Ebook]. Pennsylvania State University. https://voicesofdemocracy.umd.edu/wp-content/uploads/2010/08/hogan-steinem.pdf

James, A. (2024, January 17). *Gloria Steinem and transgender people.* Transgender Map.

https://www.transgendermap.com/issues/topics/media/gloria
-steinem/

Jensen, E. (2013, February 7). *'Gloria: in her own words,' Steinem on HBO.* The New York Times. https://www.nytimes.com/2011/08/14/arts/television/gloria-in-her-own-words-steinem-on-hbo.html

Johns, N. (2020, March 6). *At 85, why feminist icon Gloria Steinem is more woke than ever.* Footwear News. https://footwearnews.com/fashion/fashion-news/gloria-steinem-tory-burch-embrace-ambition-summit-2020-1202943616/

Karbo, K. (2019, March 25). *How Gloria Steinem became the "world's most famous feminist.* Culture. https://www.nationalgeographic.com/culture/article/how-gloria-steinem-became-worlds-most-famous-feminist?loggedin=true&rnd=1704947641627

King, S. (2019, March 8). *Steinem tries film producing: Issues come alive in Lifetime's "better off dead."* Los Angeles Times. https://www.latimes.com/archives/la-xpm-1993-01-10-tv-1331-story.html

Knox, S. (2024, February 3). *Seven things I've learned from Gloria Steinem.* Ms. Magazine. https://msmagazine.com/2011/03/25/on-her-77th-birthday-seven-things-ive-learned-from-gloria-steinem/

Kort, M. (2013, November 20). *Gloria Steinem receives top national honor.* Ms. Magazine. https://msmagazine.com/2013/11/20/gloria-steinem-receives-top-national-honor/

Kounalakis, M. (2015, October 29). *The feminist was a spy.* USC Center on Public Diplomacy. https://uscpublicdiplomacy.org/blog/feminist-was-spy

Kramer, J. (2015, October 12). *Gloria Steinem's life on the feminist frontier.* The New Yorker.

https://www.newyorker.com/magazine/2015/10/19/road-warrior-profiles-jane-kramer

Kravitz, A. (2011, June 23). *Gloria Steinem: An unheralded GLBT advocate.* Jewish Women's Archive. https://jwa.org/blog/gloria-steinem-unheralded-glbt-advocate

Leaders as guides of return: Wilma Mankiller. (2010, April 7). Women's Media Center. https://womensmediacenter.com/news-features/leaders-as-guides-of-return-wilma-mankiller

Leland, J. (2016, October 10). *What I learned about a vanished New York from Gloria Steinem.* The New York Times. https://www.nytimes.com/2016/10/10/insider/what-i-learned-about-a-vanished-new-york-from-gloria-steinem.html

Leve, A. (2024, February 18). *Gloria Steinem is still in the fight.* Esquire. https://www.esquire.com/news-politics/a46789064/gloria-steinem-profile/

Lunn, N. (2016, February 25). *12 things we learnt when Emma Watson interviewed Gloria Steinem.* Red Online. https://www.redonline.co.uk/red-women/blogs/a521911/11-things-we-learnt-when-emma-watson-interviewed-gloria-steinem

Maida, J. (2022, April 27). *Creators of take our daughters to work day reveal why boys weren't originally included.* Yahoo!Life. https://www.yahoo.com/lifestyle/the-history-of-take-our-daughters-to-work-day-130654900.html?guccounter=1

Marchese, D. (2020, September 13). *Gloria Steinem is nowhere near done with being an activist.* The New York Times. https://www.nytimes.com/interactive/2020/09/08/magazine/gloria-steinem-interview.html

Meents, M. (1972, April 28). *Interview with Pat Carbine: Co-founder of Ms. Magazine.* WNYC. https://www.wnyc.org/story/interview-with-pat-carbine-co-founder-of-ms-magazine/

Michals, D. (2017). *Gloria Steinem*. National Women's History Museum. https://www.womenshistory.org/education-resources/biographies/gloria-steinem

Miller, P. (2014, January 31). *Gloria Steinem reflects on Alice Walker documentary and her own work in India in exclusive interview*. WBAI News. https://wbai.org/articles.php?article=1722

Millett, K., Morgan, R., & Steinem, G. (1991, January 20). *Opinion | We learned the wrong lessons in Vietnam; A feminist issue still*. The New York Times. https://www.nytimes.com/1991/01/20/opinion/l-we-learned-the-wrong-lessons-in-vietnam-a-feminist-issue-still-839991.html

Mills, N. (2017, August 8). *Gloria Steinem's "a bunny's tale" – 50 years later*. The Guardian. https://www.theguardian.com/commentisfree/2013/may/26/gloria-steinem-bunny-tale-still-relevant-today

Morgan, R. (Ed.). (2003). *Sisterhood is forever: The women's anthology for a new millennium*. Atria Books. https://www.amazon.com/Sisterhood-Forever-Womens-Anthology-Millennium/dp/0743466276

Mullen, M. (2021, April 28). *Gloria Steinem publishes part one of "A Bunny's Tale" in SHOW Magazine*. HISTORY. https://www.history.com/this-day-in-history/gloria-steinem-publishes-a-bunnys-tale-show-magazine

Mullen, M. (2022, January 18). *Mahalia Jackson prompts Martin Luther King Jr. to improvise "I Have a Dream" speech*. HISTORY. https://www.history.com/this-day-in-history/mahalia-jackson-the-queen-of-gospel-puts-her-stamp-on-the-march-on-washington

Mullen-Brown, A. (2022, May 11). *"Writing is the only thing that, when I do it, it doesn't feel like I should be doing anything else."* Now Then. https://nowthenmagazine.com/articles/gloria-steinem-writing-is-the-only-thing-that-when-i-do-it-it-doesnt-feel-like-i-should-be-doing-anything-else

Napikoski, L. (2019a, February 26). *When did feminist leader Gloria Steinem get married?* ThoughtCo. https://www.thoughtco.com/when-did-gloria-steinem-get-married-3529173

Napikoski, L. (2019b, March 1). *Lavender menace: the phrase, the group, the controversy.* ThoughtCo. https://www.thoughtco.com/lavender-menace-feminism-definition-3528970

Napikoski, L. (2019c, July 3). *Articles in the first issue of Ms. Magazine.* ThoughtCo. https://www.thoughtco.com/ms-magazine-first-issue-3529076

Nicolaou, E. (2020, April 15). *Mrs. America's Gloria Steinem is still fighting for equality today.* Oprah Daily. https://www.oprahdaily.com/entertainment/tv-movies/a32121106/gloria-steinem-facts/

NPR. *At 81, feminist Gloria Steinem finds herself free of the "demands of gender."* (2015, October 26). https://www.npr.org/2015/10/26/451862822/at-81-feminist-gloria-steinem-finds-herself-free-of-the-demands-of-gender

O'Meara, M. (2021, October 19). *How Ruth Bader Ginsburg and Gloria Steinem fought for your right to get a beer.* Literary Hub. https://lithub.com/how-ruth-bader-ginsburg-and-gloria-steinem-fought-for-your-right-to-get-a-beer/

Omega Institute. (2013, October 30). *Gloria Steinem awarded Eleanor Roosevelt Val-Kill medal.* Omega. https://www.eomega.org/node/3753

Our founder. (2023, April 17). Apne Aap. https://apneaap.org/about-us/our-founder/

Our history. (2023, July 17). URGE - Unite for Reproductive & Gender Equity. https://urge.org/about/our-history-2/

Over 465 feminist leaders sign open letter standing in solidarity with transgender women and girls, including Gloria Steinem, Regina King, Halle Berry, Selena Gomez, Chelsea Clinton, Gabrielle Union, and more. (2021,

March 31). GLAAD. https://glaad.org/over-465-feminist-leaders-sign-open-letter-support-transgender-women-and-girls/

PBS. *Interview: Gloria Steinem.* (n.d.). https://www.pbs.org/kued/nosafeplace/interv/steinem.html

Rappeport, A. (2016, February 8). *Gloria Steinem and Madeleine Albright rebuke young women backing Bernie Sanders.* The New York Times. https://www.nytimes.com/2016/02/08/us/politics/gloria-steinem-madeleine-albright-hillary-clinton-bernie-sanders.html

Remarks by the President at Presidential Medal of Freedom Ceremony. (2013, November 20). White House. https://obamawhitehouse.archives.gov/the-press-office/2013/11/20/remarks-president-presidential-medal-freedom-ceremony

Research guides: Ms. magazine special collections resources. (n.d.). Smith College Libraries. https://libguides.smith.edu/c.php?g=1227509&p=8981579

Rodriguez, L. (2020, August 27). *Meghan Markle discussed voting rights and feminism with one of her biggest role models.* Global Citizen. https://www.globalcitizen.org/en/content/meghan-markle-gloria-steinem-voting-conversation/

Sargent, E. D. (2023, December 27). *Steinem arrested at embassy.* Washington Post. https://www.washingtonpost.com/archive/local/1984/12/20/steinem-arrested-at-embassy/7c74a8a3-e3e4-4618-ad92-5965f1d1fba4/

Schnall, M. (n.d.). *Timeless wisdom from Gloria Steinem.* Feminist.com. https://www.feminist.com/resources/artspeech/interviews/timeless-wisdom-from-gloria-steinem.html

Sheehy, G. (2014, October 15). *Movers and Shakers: Gloria Steinem.* Harper's BAZAAR. https://www.harpersbazaar.com/culture/features/a3984/gail-sheehy-interviews-gloria-steinem-1114/

Shelby Knox - shesource expert. (n.d.). Women's Media Center. https://womensmediacenter.com/shesource/expert/shelby-knox

Shriver, M. (2011, July 11). *Gloria Steinem.* Interview Magazine. https://www.interviewmagazine.com/culture/gloria-steinem

Silurians Press Club. (2016, April 24). *Gloria Steinem 10 top reasons for being a journalist* [Video]. YouTube. https://www.youtube.com/watch?v=QYo3zGPxfgg

Speeches: Gloria Steinem on combating sex trafficking. (2013, June 13). Apne Aap. https://apneaap.org/2012/04/speeches-gloria-steinem-on-combating-sex-trafficking/

Steinem, G. (n.d.). *Pauline Perlmutter Steinem.* Jewish Women's Archive. https://jwa.org/encyclopedia/article/steinem-pauline-perlmutter

Steinem, G. (1962, May 8). *The moral disarmament of Betty Coed.* Esquire. https://classic.esquire.com/article/1983/6/1/the-moral-disarmament-of-betty-coed

Steinem, G. (1963a). *A bunny's tale.* https://undercover.hosting.nyu.edu/files/original/5c9de8d1db51cede1395f6d6fa480ca24e872b76.pdf

Steinem, G. (1963b). *A bunny's tale: Part II.* https://sociologyinfocus.com/files/pdf/show-a%20bunny_s%20tale-part%20two-june%201963.pdf

Steinem, G. (1964). *Crazy legs or, the biography of a fashion.* Google Arts & Culture. https://artsandculture.google.com/asset/crazy-legs-or-the-biography-of-a-fashion-gloria-steinem/YgHLBZtoRhdu4g?hl=en

Steinem, G. (1969, April 4). After black power, women's liberation. *New York Magazine.* https://nymag.com/news/politics/46802/

Steinem, G. (1970, August 31). *What it would be like if women win.* TIME. https://content.time.com/time/subscriber/article

Steinem, G. (1994, June 4). *Moving beyond words.* Simon & Schuster. https://www.amazon.com/Moving-Beyond-Words-Gloria-Steinem/dp/0671649728

Steinem, G. (1998, April 6). *30th anniversary issue / Gloria Steinem: first feminist.* New York Magazine. https://nymag.com/nymetro/news/people/features/2438/

Steinem, G. (2004, September). *Leaps of consciousness.* Feminist.com. https://www.feminist.com/resources/artspeech/genwom/leaps.html

Steinem, G. (2008, January 9). *Opinion | Women are never front-runners.* The New York Times. https://www.nytimes.com/2008/01/08/opinion/08steinem.html

Steinem, G. (2010, December 15). *Fond farewells: Wilma Mankiller.* TIME. https://content.time.com/time/specials/packages/article/0,28804,2036683_2036477_2036470,00.html

Steinem, G. (2015, October 27). *My life on the road.* Random House. https://www.amazon.com/My-Life-Road-Gloria-Steinem/dp/0345408160

Steinem, G. (2015, November 17). *Op-ed: On working together over time.* Advocate.com. https://www.advocate.com/commentary/2013/10/02/op-ed-working-together-over-time

Steinem, G. (2017, July 15). *I'm a hopeaholic. There's nothing George Bush can do about it.* The Guardian. https://www.theguardian.com/world/2005/sep/13/usa.comment

Steinem, G. (2020, September 28). "What would Ruth do?": A feminist pioneer on what Justice Ginsburg meant to her. *SCOTUSblog.* https://www.scotusblog.com/2020/09/what-would-ruth-do-a-feminist-pioneer-on-what-justice-ginsburg-meant-to-her/

Steinem, G. (2020, November). *Gloria Steinem | Speaker*. TED Talks. https://www.ted.com/speakers/gloria_steinem

Steinem, G. (2021). *Gloria Steinem: Princess of Asturias Award for Communication and Humanities 2021*. The Princess of Asturias Foundation. https://www.fpa.es/en/princess-of-asturias-awards/laureates/2021-gloria-steinem.html?texto=discurso&especifica=0

Steinem, G. (2022, July 7). *Gloria Steinem: Why it's so important to be a passionate voter*. Cosmopolitan. https://www.cosmopolitan.com/politics/news/a32587/gloria-steinem-passionate-voter/

Steinem, G. (2023, January 5). *We live as long as we are remembered*. Women's Media Center. https://womensmediacenter.com/news-features/we-live-as-long-as-we-are-remembered-gloria-steinem-remembers-dorothy-pitman-hughes

Steinem, G. (2023, September 20). *We are not alone: 50 years of Ms. magazine*. Literary Hub. https://lithub.com/we-are-not-alone-50-years-of-ms-magazine/

Steinem, G., & Scott, L. M. (2003). Interview with Gloria Steinem. *Advertising & Society Review, 4*(4). https://doi.org/10.1353/asr.2003.0021

Stogsdill, S. (2010, April 8). *Gloria Steinem reflects on friendship with Wilma Mankiller*. Oklahoman. https://www.oklahoman.com/story/news/politics/2010/04/08/gloria-steinem-reflects-on-friendship-with-wilma-mankiller/61264327007/

Susman, C. (2004, March 27). *Steinem reminisces about late husband, envisions her future*. The Ledger. https://www.theledger.com/story/news/2004/03/27/steinem-reminisces-about-late-husband-envisions-her-future/26106870007/

Talcott, M. (2020, July 17). *We heart: Gloria Steinem's powerful call to action.* Ms. Magazine. https://msmagazine.com/2020/07/17/we-heart-gloria-steinems-powerful-call-to-action/

She's nobody's baby: The history of American women in the 20th century. (2021, May 18). The Peabody Awards. https://peabodyawards.com/award-profile/shes-nobodys-baby-the-history-of-american-women-in-the-20th-century/

The story of Apne Aap. (2020, May 8). Apne Aap. https://apneaap.org/about-us/the-story-of-apne-aap/

Tignor, S. (2021, March 31). *Decades later, Renée Richards' breakthrough is as important as ever.* Tennis. https://www.tennis.com/news/articles/decades-later-renee-richards-breakthrough-is-as-important-as-ever

Tranter, K. (2015, October 21). *Gloria Steinem: Still steinemite!* The Sydney Morning Herald. https://www.smh.com.au/lifestyle/gloria-steinem-still-steinemite-20151008-gk47ii.html

Truffaut-Wong, O. (2017, August 22). *How Gloria Steinem & Dolores Huerta championed intersectionality in activism.* Bustle. https://www.bustle.com/p/how-gloria-steinem-dolores-huerta-championed-intersectionality-in-activism-video-77951

Tucker, R. (2015, November 30). *"We come to feminism in different ways": Gloria Steinem on a lifetime of travels.* National Post. https://nationalpost.com/entertainment/books/we-come-to-feminism-in-different-ways-gloria-steinem-on-a-lifetime-of-travels

UN Story. (2023, November 23). *Gloria Steinem: The link between women's rights and peace* [Video]. YouTube. https://www.youtube.com/watch?v=uqNscDvkX1s

Vinopal, C. (2020, August 18). *Gloria Steinem on the role of women of color in the suffrage movement.* PBS NewsHour.

https://www.pbs.org/newshour/nation/gloria-stcincm-on the-role-of-women-of-color-in-the-suffrage-movement

Vogue India (2016, September 30). *Gloria Steinem talks about feminism, her life journey and what it means to be a woman in today's world.* Vogue India. https://www.vogue.in/content/gloria-steinem-young-women-today-are-more-shit-free-than-we-were

Voros, D. (1993, July 13). *America undercover multiple personalities: The search for deadly memories.* Variety. https://variety.com/1993/tv/reviews/america-undercover-multiple-personalities-the-search-for-deadly-memories-1200432783/

Waxman, O. B. (2017, April 26). *The inside story of why take your daughter to work day exists.* TIME. https://time.com/4753128/take-your-our-daughters-to-work-day-history/

Whittier, N. (2002). Persistence and Transformation: Gloria Steinem, The Women's Action Alliance, and the Feminist Movement, 1971-1997. *Journal of Women's History, 14*(2), 148–150. https://doi.org/10.1353/jowh.2002.0059

Woman. (n.d.). Viceland. https://www.vicetv.com/en_us/show/woman

Written Works. (n.d.). Gloria Steinem. http://www.gloriasteinem.com/written-works

Printed in Great Britain
by Amazon

47979336R00078